...but it's also the beginning.

'If our world held the feminine mysteries at the center as the true beginning place – the way it was meant to be – *Your Soul Had a Dream, Your Life Is It* would be how we knew to live. A potent and illuminating guide for this journey of remembering our way home.'
TAMI LYNN KENT, AUTHOR OF *WILD FEMININE*, *WILD CREATIVE*, AND *WILD MOTHERING*

'With courage forged in the fires of ancient rage and words formed in the clarity of a wholly loving heart, Rebecca bares her soul with raw grace. This book will comfort you and inspire you. It will light your way through the darkest landscape and sing you into the light.'
BINNIE A. DANSBY, FOUNDER OF THE SOURCE PROCESS AND BREATHWORK HEALING SYSTEM

'Welcome to your new life! When it feels like your ego is dying, it's because your soul is being born. In Rebecca Campbell's brilliant new book, she acts as a spiritual midwife, sharing all her magical skills and experience to help you give birth to even more of your True Self.'
ROBERT HOLDEN, AUTHOR OF *SHIFT HAPPENS!* AND *HIGHER PURPOSE*

'*Your Soul Had a Dream, Your Life Is It* is an invitation for depth Soulcrafting by one of our beloved modern mystics. Through her intimate sharing of awakening and transformation, Rebecca tracks and weaves the magic and mysteries dear to my heart – the effect of our birth imprint and the transformational power of birthing. This book is a treasure.'
JANE HARDWICKE COLLINGS, AUTHOR AND FOUNDER OF THE SCHOOL OF SHAMANIC WOMANCRAFT

'The longer I have known Rebecca, the deeper and more mystical she has become. People talk about walking the spiritual path and developing practice – Rebecca has allowed her entire life to be entwined with the work that she has felt called to share. This book will take you to the depth's of your soul so that you can emerge, so that you can unfurl, and so that you can bloom too.'
KYLE GRAY, BEST-SELLING AUTHOR OF *RAISE YOUR VIBRATION*

'A profound guide for anyone moving through a long and dark night of the Soul. Through storytelling and sacred teachings, Rebecca weaves the extremes of life – tomb and womb, sorrow and sweetness, rising and falling and rising again. I have never read a book that speaks with such depth, experience, and compassion about the immense, challenging, ecstatic, and heart-wrenching experience it can be to remember the Soul's dream and courageously bring it forth on Earth.'
MADELINE GILES, AUTHOR OF *THEN I WOKE UP*

'What Rebecca has created here is soul medicine of my favorite variety. The kind that rather than attempting to universalize an experience invites us into our own contemplations and activations.'
ELIZABETH DIALTO, FOUNDER OF THE SCHOOL OF SACRED EMBODIMENT AND HOST OF THE *EMBODIED* PODCAST

'Rebecca Campbell's insightful exploration of our journey through life is nothing short of transformative. With her unique blend of wisdom and compassion, she guides readers through the intricate phases of a life, offering profound insights and practical guidance. Her eloquent prose and deep understanding of the human experience make this book a must-read for anyone seeking to navigate the ebbs and flows of life with grace and purpose.'
SHAWN LEONARD, AUTHOR OF *SPIRIT TALKER*

'A powerful book that not only reminds you of your divine magnificence, but also leads you there with love.'
BRONNIE WARE, AUTHOR OF *THE TOP FIVE REGRETS OF THE DYING*

'*Your Soul Had a Dream, Your Life Is It* is part prayer, invitation and initiation. Sharing her own potent and pivotal personal experiences, Rebecca Campbell illuminates the portal welcoming us when we inquire and listen within. This book is a reminder to stay open, curious, and connected. It's a true gem I will return to again and again.'
NANCY LEVIN, AUTHOR OF *EMBRACE YOUR SHADOW TO FIND YOUR LIGHT*

'An essential guide for anyone devoted to their soul's path and the mystery and magic therein. Rebecca puts words to mystical experiences I've had but never really knew how to talk about. This book has helped make them real for me.'
KATE NORTHRUP, BEST-SELLING AUTHOR OF AUTHOR OF *DO LESS*

'I felt so alive reading this book. Rebecca has a unique gift that takes you on a journey of life and all existence. She captures the rhythm of breath and life that celebrates your soul and who you are, why you are here.'
ANNABELLE SHARMAN, AUTHOR OF *THE FUTURE ANCESTOR*

'Rebecca's latest creation speaks right into the heart of the times we are in, providing solace and guidance during times of great transformation and meaning to why we are here. Such powerful work for a time of a crisis of meaning and a need to return to the soul.'
ALEXANDRA ROXO, BEST-SELLING AUTHOR OF *F*CK LIKE A GODDESS* AND *DARE TO FEEL*

## ALSO BY REBECCA CAMPBELL

**Books and Audiobooks**
Letters to a Starseed
Rise Sister Rise
Light Is the New Black

**Oracle Card Decks**
The Ancient Stones Oracle
The Healing Waters Oracle
The Rose Oracle
Work Your Light Oracle Cards
The Starseed Oracle

**Certification Trainings and Courses**
Oracle Card Reader Certification with Rebecca Campbell
The Inner Temple Mystery School Accredited Training
Healing the Mother Line
Mysteries of the Rose Workshop
*and more!*

**Meditations, Rituals, Soul Journeys, Classes, and Chants**
**Available on rebeccacampbell.me**
Your Ancient Past Lives
Discover Your Spirit Guides
Energetic Protection
Healing Is Happening
The Great Mother
*and more!*

REBECCA CAMPBELL

# your
# SOUL
## had a dream
# your
# LIFE

how to be held by
life when it feels like
everything is falling apart

# is it

**HAY HOUSE**

Carlsbad, California • New York City
London • Sydney • New Delhi

**Published in the United Kingdom by:**
Hay House UK Ltd, The Sixth Floor, Watson House,
54 Baker Street, London W1U 7BU
Tel: +44 (0)20 3927 7290; www.hayhouse.co.uk

**Published in the United States of America by:**
Hay House LLC, PO Box 5100, Carlsbad, CA 92018-5100
Tel: (1) 760 431 7695 or (800) 654 5126; www.hayhouse.com

**Published in Australia by:**
Hay House Publishing Australia Pty Ltd, 18/36 Ralph St, Alexandria NSW 2015
Tel: (61) 2 9669 4299; www.hayhouse.com.au

**Published in India by:**
Hay House Publishers (India) Pvt Ltd, Muskaan Complex,
Plot No.3, B-2, Vasant Kunj, New Delhi 110 070
Tel: (91) 11 4176 1620; www.hayhouse.co.in

Text © Rebecca Campbell, 2024

The moral rights of the author have been asserted.

The information given in this book should not be treated as a substitute for professional medical advice; always consult a medical practitioner. Any use of information in this book is at the reader's discretion and risk. Neither the author nor the publisher can be held responsible for any loss, claim or damage arising out of the use, or misuse, of the suggestions made, the failure to take medical advice or for any material on third-party websites.

A catalogue record for this book is available from the British Library.

Hardcover ISBN: 978-1-78817-516-6
Ebook ISBN: 978-1-78817-545-6
Audiobook ISBN: 978-1-78817-614-9

Images: Endpaper artwork by Katie-Louise; p.8: © Rebecca Campbell and Danielle Noel

10 9 8 7 6 5 4 3 2 1

Printed in the United States of America

This product uses responsibly sourced papers and/or recycled materials. For more information, see www.hayhouse.com.

*For Craig, Sunny, and Goldie,*
*who invited me to incarnate*
*so much more deeply than before.*

# CONTENTS

## PART TWO: YOU'RE GOING SOMEWHERE SACRED
*Understanding That Change Is Part of Life and Healing*
*Is Always Happening*

## PART THREE: THE WAY OF THE MYSTIC
*Reconnecting to the Spirit of Life and Walking Your Sacred Path*

# △
# DEEPENING YOUR
# READING EXPERIENCE

My vision for *Your Soul Had a Dream, Your Life Is It* goes further than the book itself. You'll find several free resources to deepen your reading experience at rebeccacampbell.me/yoursoulhadadream, including...

## Free Guided Workbook

A special dedicated workbook full of all of the Soul Inquiry journaling prompts featured throughout the book.

## Meditations, Chant, and Playlist

Listen to the Unbound chant, meditations, and playlist mentioned in the book for free!

## #YourSoulHadADream

I love seeing your beautiful book pics; tag me at @rebeccacampbell_author using #YourSoulHadADream

# △
# INTRODUCTION

This is a book about change that was written during a period of great change, within me and within the world. Who I was when I started it is unrecognizable from who I am today. No part of me is the same. Stoked in the initiatory fires of mid-life, becoming a mother, a global pandemic, and the dark nights of the soul, only the most potent embers remain.

Perhaps you've gone through something similar, too. Navigating the changing seasons of your life and your soul's own darkest nights. Or maybe you're there right now, in the messy gunk of your own transformation. Not quite who you once were, and not quite who you'll soon be. In the muddy rubble of your life. In the in-between. Half one thing, half the next. Your soul scheduled to go deeper than before...

The dark nights of the soul is an initiatory period in our spiritual awakening journey that tends to follow the earlier stages of illumination and heightened spiritual experiences that I call the ascent. The dark nights of the soul is the descent. It's the contraction before the expansion. The separation before the union. The winter before the spring. The tomb before the womb. It's the birth canal in which we rebirth ourselves, often right in the middle of our lives.

During the descent, our soul is invited to incarnate deeper than before, and while every soul journey is unique, it's often during the darkest nights that we're brought face-to-face with what's been lain dormant. I refer to it as dark *nights* rather than *night* because this period seems to last much longer than we expect. For me, this part of the spiritual awakening journey has been the most difficult to navigate, and it's hurled me deep into my body, my ancestry, the Earth, and humanity.

This is a book about rebirth. Which means it's a book about death, for rebirth isn't possible without it. This is a book about healing. Which means it's also about feeling, for healing isn't possible without it. This is a book about finding yourself. Which means it's also about losing yourself, for finding yourself isn't possible without it.

Life is always trying to initiate us into who we're becoming. It's nature's way, and it always involves *change*. Change is the one constant in life, and every moment of every day nature shows us how to embrace change. Nature is the greatest mystery school there is. The snake knows, the rose hip does too, that we need to surrender what once was to one day be born anew.

Of all my books, this one has asked the most of me and it's taken more than seven years to complete. I wrote it during a unique period in my life in which I was pregnant three times and welcomed two babies into the world – one did not make it past the second trimester. Much of the book came to me and through me while soul was being woven into matter and my entire body was expanding and contracting.

In 2017, I had two spontaneous mystical experiences in which I was shown the gates of Life – birth and death – and how this life is a mere breath in the existence of the soul. These awakening experiences, which took me many years to integrate, transmitted something deep into my cells and changed the trajectory of my life.

My intention in this book is to use the initiatory gateways of birth and death – as well as others, including loss, love, beginnings and endings – as metaphors to describe how we can navigate the change, transformation, healing, and rebirth that we're all going through, both individually and collectively. And to acknowledge the great initiation that our souls went through to be here right now.

For some reason, beyond the surface details of 'what happened,' birth and death are rarely discussed in a deep way that acknowledges how huge they are for us as initiations. This fascinates me; why aren't we talking more about these profound experiences that are so deeply ingrained in nature? Perhaps we find it hard to do so because of their enormity, or because we're afraid of the unknown. I believe that metaphorically, the great initiations of birth and death hold much wisdom that can help us to transform and truly live. I wonder, could they hold the codes to transformation and a possible rebirth for humanity?

I want to acknowledge the complexities and sensitivities surrounding some of the subjects featured in this book – particularly pregnancy, birth, postpartum, baby loss (in the *Rebirthed* and *The Birth Mysteries* chapters), ancestral healing, intergenerational healing, trauma, and spiritual emergency – and hold space and compassion for our differing experiences of them.

If any of the topics I touch on are difficult or painful for you, I encourage you to listen to what you need. And while no two journeys are the same, I've included a list of some of the resources that I personally found helpful on pages 260–62; however, always trust how you are led. I believe that by sharing our stories in ways that feel safe, we allow space for healing to happen and help one another feel less alone.

Throughout the book, you'll find references to the 'Great Mother,' 'Goddess,' 'Cosmic Mother,' 'Original Mother,' and the 'Ancient Grandmothers of the Earth.' These terms are related to my two mystical experiences in 2017, and to the part of my journey into which they initiated me, which I call the descent and a Great Mother awakening. My intention in sharing them is to convey the comfort I experienced in reconnecting with these deeply ancient sacred feminine energies of the Earth and the cosmos. And to potentially transmit this energy through these pages.

I also use words and phrases that attempt to encapsulate the ineffable Spirit of Life – including 'spirit,' 'the intelligent pulse of Life,' 'life-force,' 'sacred,' 'cosmos,' 'great mystery,' 'the Unseen Spirit of Life,' and 'God.' If these terms don't resonate with you, please substitute them with your own.

Another word you'll find is 'mystic.' A mystic is someone who longs to experience life as sacred and actively seeks the sacred that's here all around us and within us. They long to have a direct and physical experience of the divine, deep in their body, which is a path of awakening that's available to us all. They see nature as a great teacher and long to experience it intimately and deeply. The path of the mystic is the path of the heart – no matter how difficult life gets, the mystic yearns to experience it all and to keep their heart open.

I believe that there's no greater intelligence than the wisdom within and nothing more powerful than acting on it, and so at the end of many chapters, you'll find Soul Inquiry® prompts that will help you hear the calls of your soul as you read the book. Don't underestimate the power of these prompts. I recommend journaling on them or even grabbing a pen and writing directly onto these pages. Don't overthink it, just write whatever comes – the answers your soul gives have the potential to change your life. You can find a free downloadable and printable pdf with all of the prompts from the book (*see page xiii*).

The words I share in the book come from my own limited lived experience. As a western woman born in Australia and with Irish, British, Nordic, Icelandic, and German ancestry, I've been on a deep journey of reconnecting with the Indigenous traditions of my lineage. I've also studied and have a great appreciation of and reverence for traditions which are not my own ancestrally but have still deeply touched me. I write with good intentions for all in my heart, but also acknowledge my biases, limitations, and humanness. I hope you feel the tenderness behind my words as you read them.

Your soul chose a *powerful* time to be alive. However, it's not an *easy* time to be alive. The planet is changing and so is humanity. And we know it needs to. So much that's been hidden and lain dormant is coming to the surface for us to witness, within ourselves and the collective. We've been sobered and broken open by the ways that humans have separated off from one another and the Earth.

In these cycle-breaking times, so many of us have been experiencing deep ancestral healing and clearing. Some are processing the trauma of their childhoods and lives, while others are also processing things for their ancestral lines and the collective. And some are integrating it all. These are the cycle breakers, and since you're reading this, maybe you're one of them.

I wonder if this is a necessary part of our evolution as a species. Is there an intelligence within what each of us is experiencing now, during what some feel is a collective dark night of the soul? Is this a normal part of the spiritual journey, or are we experiencing it in increasingly different ways to the generations that came before? Is this part of a collective rebirth for humanity? Everyone's journey here on Earth is unique. To incarnate at this time is a courageous thing to do. We each hold a thread for the healing of humanity. Don't underestimate the one you're holding.

My wish is that this book meets you where you are and makes you feel a little less alone as you navigate the great dream of your soul to be here now. That it stokes the embers of your soul's inextinguishable light through its darkest nights and initiatory gateways.

I hope that it encourages you to stay connected to your mystical heart and to gather the courage to keep it open through all the extremes that this life brings. That it helps you to feel held by Life and to see the beauty woven through it all, especially when it's hard to see it. That it helps you to embrace the ever-changing seasons of your life. And that when the time comes – and you'll *know* when – you release your petals to the wind for the chance to do it again and again.

Love,

Rebecca

Your life is but a b r e a t h
in the existence of your soul,
and incarnating here at this time
is such a courageous thing to do.

**Your soul had a dream,**
**and your life, this life, is it.**

*Part One*

# THE END
## *is also the*
# BEGINNING

*Navigating Life's Initiatory
Gateways and Darkest Nights*

# △
# FALL INTO MY ARMS

In 2017 I had a spontaneous mystical, unitive experience that would leave me forever changed. As I rode the Tube to my kirtan teacher training in West London, I had no idea that my soul was scheduled to go deeper than ever before.

Kirtan is a key practice in Bhakti yoga, the yoga of devotion, and for weeks, we'd been learning about the rebellious poet-saints of ancient India, singing the name of the divine, and chanting sacred Sanskrit mantras passed down through the ages. It was a mystic's dream to be merging with the sacred day after day. My fellow students are a rare kind of devotional, longing to intimately experience union with the divine and fascinated by the ancient science of sound. Basking in the original sounds of the cosmos was a kind of heaven I'd always dreamed of but never knew existed.

On this particular day, we were completing a two-day exercise led by my teacher and friend Nikki Slade. Gathered in a circle, we took turns to stand in its center while the other students tried to knock us off kilter by using both criticism and praise. The student in the center had to sing their way back to the divine while navigating the jagged rocks of criticism and praise, in order to be a clear channel for the divine to work through them.

The moment I stepped into the center of the circle, I felt that something significant was about to happen. Without warning, and mid sound and movement, my body froze, and I was unable to move. As Nikki checked that I was okay, I could feel the veil to the unseen world of spirit becoming thin. I heard clear instructions, which I relayed to the group: 'I'm being told I need to use my voice to let Shakti move through what's been frozen. But to do so, I need the space to be held. Is the space held?'

Nikki instructed the class and said that the space was held. Then, as I stood in the center of the circle, my hands moved forward several times, parting the veil like a ballerina dancing on stage. Suddenly, in one swooping movement, my arms and torso flung up and down, up and down, as I entered a trance-like state.

My consciousness hurtled to the center of the Earth, and I found myself in an ancient pool of primordial water being cradled in the arms of a presence of the Great Cosmic Mother, Original Mother, Great Mother of us all. I hadn't consciously seen Her before this moment and yet she felt deeply familiar, as if I'd always known her. She caressed my face, rocking me, soothing me, singing to me and through me.

I looked up and was shown the gates of Life, which all souls enter when we take our first breath and exit when we exhale our last. I saw that everything in the cosmos is held together by an intelligent pulse, through the beating of our hearts and the inhale and exhale of our breath. I saw that this life is a mere stitch in the tapestry of our soul's journey and that all who are on Earth now chose to be here, at this pivotal moment of change, healing, and possible rebirth for humanity. In the heavens above was a canopy of stars in a black cosmic sky that went on forever.

While I was being cradled in the arms of the Great Cosmic Mother – who I experienced like the most fertile soil and the vast night sky, an experience of comfort and blackness, and as both ancient and timeless, familiar yet mysterious – I was surrounded by a group of ancient beings, a collective consciousness who introduced themselves as the Ancient Grandmothers of the Earth. Made of the Earth and the cosmos. Star and soil. Ancient and future. Guardians of the sacred waters of this planet. Ancient ancestors of us all, keepers of the Earth. Connecting us all through our ancestry to the Original Mother of us all.

They each sang ancient songs through the ages to all of humanity. Unbroken, vibrational songs.

It was the most intimate, sensual experience, with more love, sweetness, compassion, understanding, and holding than I ever thought was possible. Receiving this love, tenderness, and witnessing satiated a hunger, a separation, a grief deep within me that I'd always felt yet was unable to name.

The Grandmothers then began singing to me and through me. Songs, words, and melodies I'd never heard before sang through me in languages I didn't know. (Later, when I shared this experience with Yeye Teish, a spiritual teacher for whom I have deep respect, she told me about xenoglossy, a phenomenon in which one can speak and understand a language without having prior knowledge of it. Some say this is the soul connecting with past lives; others believe that the language is being channeled from the ancient consciousness held in the memory of the Earth.)

The Great Cosmic Mother soothed my soul, as if to say, 'We know this human journey can be hard. That the separation we all feel is at times excruciating. How difficult it can be not to know that you're held in our arms, and not to feel held by the sacred Spirit of Life while you're here on Earth. But we've never left you and at any moment you can return to the sacred pulse of Life. Through reconnecting with the sacred pulse of the Earth you'll connect with the sacred pulse of the cosmos. The sacred is woven here on Earth just as deeply as it is in heaven.'

The Grandmothers showed me my ancestral line, and all our ancestral lines. I saw how long our disconnection from the Divine Feminine, from the Earth, has been going on and how this disconnection from Her has resulted in so much grief and disconnection within humanity. And I understood that until we reconnect with Her, we'll remain separate, both individually and as a species.

They showed me all the trauma, pain, and harm that this separation has caused. They showed me how all the souls who choose to come at this time are part of the collective cellular healing of humanity on Earth. How each soul holds a different thread for the healing and evolution of humanity.

I was shown that when we close off our hearts to protect ourselves from the pain of life, we also close ourselves off from the joy and the sweetness. And that to experience the ecstasy we also need to experience the agony; all of this is part of the adventure of Life. We need to embrace autumn (fall) and winter just as much as spring and summer: these feminine seasons have so much wisdom and nectar for us too.

I traveled through my maternal ancestral line, all the way back to the Original Mother, the mother of us all. She had held me through all the heartbreaks and all the severings in my life, in my mother's life, in her mother's (my grandmother's) life and so on, all the way back to the beginning. She showed me all the births and all the deaths.

She assured me that this whole time she'd never left my side (nor anyone else's). As if to say, 'I know that the human experience can be challenging for the soul, but it's also sweet. Don't shut yourself off from it. Remember why your soul chose to come.' It was the most beautiful, compassionate, sensual, and tender moment of my life, one that's deeply imprinted within my cells. I can still touch and taste it now.

I took a deep breath and felt my torso rise and fall as my consciousness traveled up from the watery caverns at the center of the Earth and into the room in a studio on a busy street in West London. As I came out of the spontaneous trance state, eyes still closed, I could feel myself slowly moving back through the veil and I could sense the holding of my classmates.

Nikki explained to the class that we'd just experienced something deeply sacred, and she instructed them to give me space as I integrated it. We did our closing chant, and my body shook as the Shakti energy physically traveled up and down my spine and then throughout my entire body. (Shakti is the Sanskrit word for the spiritual cosmic energy of the Divine Feminine.) I experienced being showered by codes of light right into my cells, as if heaven was merging with the Earth and something ancient was being awakened and activated deep within me.

During the lunch break that followed, a fellow student spoke with me about one of the songs she'd heard me sing while in the trance; she knew it as an ancient Goddess chant from her lineage, which was different from my own. Later, at home, I listened to a recording of that chant, and while I'd never heard it before and wasn't even aware of the Goddess to whom it was devoted, I couldn't deny that this was one of the songs I'd sung.

Amazed by what had happened that day, and unsure where to even begin to process it, I went to bed. But the Great Mother continued to move through me; it was the first of the visits from her and the Ancient Grandmothers that would continue every night for many months.

This mystical experience with the Great Mother propelled me into a relentless, deeply physical journey of healing – ancestral, societal, cultural, and personal – in which I was forced to look at the ways I'd denied the feminine, pushed down my anger or grief, attempted to bypass my own humanity, projected God onto anyone or anything outside of myself, and become disconnected from the Earth as sacred.

Not quite ready to share the details of my mystical experience with the world, I dove into creating oracle card decks as a way of bringing the transmission and visions of it into form. This artwork for the 'Fall into My Arms' card in *The Starseed Oracle* (which I co-created with Danielle Noel) is one of the pieces based on this mystical trance experience.

*Fall into My Arms*

It would take me many years to find the words to speak about my mystical experience with the Great Mother and Grandmothers. These are those words, and this is that story.

Throughout the years that followed, I continued to receive teachings directly from the Great Mother and these have completely transformed the way I live my life and see the dream our soul had to be here now. I share them here with you as offerings, so that no matter how dark it gets or how much it feels as if life is falling apart, you'll feel a little less alone with nothing to hold you. May these pages help you to remember the dream your soul had before you chose to come.

# △
# HELD

The Great Cosmic Mother ushered you in when you took your first breath and she'll be there when you exhale your last. She knows how challenging life on Earth can be. That at times, being human can be painful, lonely, and confusing. That the polarity and separation can be difficult when your soul remembers the oneness of Source. But at the same time, it can be incredibly ecstatic, glorious, and sweet.

We often see things as either good or bad: when things go well, we make it mean that everything's okay; and when things don't work out, then perhaps we've done something wrong or have something to fix. We've forgotten that life on Earth isn't like that. Polarity is at the core of the Earth experience. And it's through the polar extremes that we grow the most. We're not meant to avoid the night, the shadow, the winter, and the fall. Indeed, the union you seek will be found through the portal of the polarity that so many of us are trying so hard to avoid.

This life is but a single breath in the inextinguishable existence of your experience as a soul. Hand over your worries, your hurt, your sorrows, fears, and doubts to the Great Cosmic Mother, the great mystery of Life. Lay them on Her altar. Return to the sureness of the soil. Fall fully into Her arms.

Remember that your cells are made of Her ancient exploded stars; the flowers are too. And that while these extremes are difficult, they can also be magnificent. Unbridled joy and love are closer to grief than you think. And perhaps, the more wildly the pendulum of your life swings in these initiatory rebirthing times, the more you can say: 'I've truly lived.'

# great mother activation

I'm ready to embrace the extremes of this human life.
I soften and open my heart to it all and through it all.
I say yes to the expansion and the depths.
I surrender to my soul's wildest dream.

I lay all that I'm carrying onto Her altar
and fall into the Great Mother's arms.

# △
# LIFE'S INITIATORY GATEWAYS

*'My soul is the bridge between spirit and body, and as such,
is a uniter of opposites. Without soul at the center, I would
either transcend into spirit or become mired in matter.'*

MARION WOODMAN

When our souls choose to experience a life here on Earth, there are two initiations that we all share, no matter who we are: birth and death. These initiations are what unite us, and you'll find the secrets of Life and rebirth encoded there.

We all come from the dark, watery world of a biological mother before we make our entrance into this world. Her body is the portal in which our soul gestates and travels through. As we grow, each of us and our journeys are unique.

Is our life path and its circumstances consciously chosen or predestined by the soul? Did we dream of being here? And when, oh when, will we draw our last breath and travel beyond? These are the great mysteries of birth and death. These are the great mysteries of human life on Earth.

The soul is what makes life possible for us. It's our inextinguishable, unique essence. The spark of life that's present when we take our first breath and continues after we exhale our last. Without the soul, 'we' would not exist here. You need only see a body after the soul has left it to know that what animated that person is no more. All that remains is a vessel of matter, bones, organs, hair, and flesh. Life has left. Soul is not here. Soon this vehicle will decompose; without the soul at the center, the part that makes us who we are is no longer here.

What if the purpose of life is to welcome more and more of our soul here? In every cell of our bodies. And the more of our soul we welcome in, the more life-force we have and the more 'ourselves' we become. Is this what it means to say yes to being reborn in the middle of our lives? Is this what the shamans meant when they spoke of 'dying while still fully living'?

Each time we *awaken* we allow more of our soul and life-force to be here, in this life, in this body, on this planet, at this time. Each time we *change*, we're given this opportunity. To *expand*: to allow life to open us and let more life-force in. Each time we *grieve* we're given this opportunity. To let life stretch our heart wider open. To expand: to open and let more life in. Each time we're *challenged* we're given this opportunity. To expand, to open and let more life in. All through our lives, we're invited to awaken and then expand and open to let more life-force, more soul, more spirit in. The one constant in life, *change*, is the great driver of this expansion, but we need to say yes to it.

> *A birth, a death, a love, a loss, a discovery, an ending, a beginning – at these initiatory gateways we're invited to let life change us, expand us, and open us: spiritually, emotionally, mentally, and physically.*

This is easier said than done, though, because for transformation to take place (for to change *is* to transform), we must be willing to loosen our grip on the way things were and allow a rebirth to happen. At life's initiatory gateways we're given a choice: to say yes to change and transformation or to shut off from it. To surrender to the great mystery of life or attempt to control it. To open our minds to the unknown mystery of life or close off in an attempt to find certainty.

One choice will expand us, increase our life-force, and invite spirit to come more fully in. The other will shut us down, harden our hearts, close our minds, and decrease our life-force. Every time we say yes to change, we expand and awaken a little bit more. More light comes into our physical body, and our cells, mind, and heart need to expand to receive it. As this happens there's often a period of purging and purification in which it can feel like we're going backward, but in reality, nothing could be further from the truth.

And I've noticed that with every expansion comes a corresponding contraction as we prepare ourselves to embody and integrate the change that's occurred. At this time of contraction, we must mourn that which was in order for that which will be to be born. And through surrender, through embodiment, we become more and more ourselves as more and more of the soul sinks into the cells. And as it does so, the more intimately and physically we're able to experience the divine. We truly become the bridge between heaven and Earth to meet and merge.

The awakening journey is not for the weak or closed-hearted. It's the path of the tender, open, mystical, creative, intuitive heart. It comes without an external map, and we're called to be led from the sacred pulse within. The one sure guide is Life itself. And the good news is that you are part of Life itself, for you are part of nature, and nature knows how to expand and awaken. It's never stagnant or resistant to change and transformation. It knows how to surrender what it once was to the Earth for the chance to do it again. Rebirth is in its blueprint. And because you are nature, rebirth is in your blueprint too.

## SOUL INQUIRY

*How are you changing right now?*

# the core of who she was was in transition

Half one thing, half the next.
The breaking down was necessary.

The petals of the blooms that
once captivated others,
returning to the Earth,
to the Earth, to the Earth.

Transformation was imminent.
Future selves beckoned her to surrender
to the cloak of the darkest night.

Her soul was scheduled to go deeper than ever before.

# △
# THE ASCENT: AWAKENING OF THE MIND, HEART, AND BODY

The planet is awakening. It's coming online. Humanity is changing. Transforming. Evolving. And it needs to. You're part of this evolution. But awakening and healing are not easy or pretty. There's an up and a down. An ascent and a descent. Expansion is followed by contraction, and contraction is followed by expansion, and if we truly surrender, there's a rebirth. It's nature's way. Transformation is the most natural thing in the world. But it's not possible without something ending first, and that requires surrendering to the unknown.

Is our awakening process changing along with the planet? Or are there ancient principles and stages that we can track and map? While no two soul paths are the same, and the awakening journey never ends, from my own lived experience, and through witnessing those of thousands of others, I've come to see that the awakening process tends to begin with a succession of upward openings that I call the ascent.

The ascent involves an expansion or awakening of the mind, the heart, and the body, which together create an opening that invites the soul to incarnate, to enter matter, a little deeper than before. Through the expansions of the ascent, we may experience universal revelations, spiritual visions, heightened psychic abilities, deep connection, unity consciousness, interconnectedness, unconditional love, and even bouts of ecstasy and bliss. And through their corresponding contractions we may experience more seemingly negative states as we process what's being cleared from our physical, emotional, and spiritual bodies.

## AWAKENING OF THE MIND

For many, the first stage of the awakening process is an upward expansion of consciousness; this phase is associated with the intellect and the conscious mind. All of a sudden, we see the world through new eyes. We unplug from what we were told is true and plug into a different, more interconnected consciousness. We see our place in the cosmos and question the meaning of life. But all this is from a mind understanding rather than a deep inner knowing.

We shift from living in an unconscious trance into something much more conscious. It feels like a whole new world has awoken, and in some ways it has. But really, we're just waking up and opening our eyes to see things more deeply as they are. This stage can trigger what I call the dark night of the mind or ego. The world isn't what you thought it was, and so you need to create new, more stable ground to build your life on.

Mind awakening may seem like a destination at which you've arrived or will arrive at once you understand this new consciousness through the gathering of information. But as you cling on to that, eventually the winds of change come a-blowing and you realize that awakening is a journey not a destination and that journey never ends. You've only just begun and the more you think you know, the less you actually do.

## AWAKENING OF THE HEART

The deeper you travel along your awakening journey, the more easily you're able to drop into your heart. The heart is the home of the soul; it's the bridge between heaven and Earth. It's the first organ to develop and when it stops beating our human form is no longer. When your heart awakens you discover who you truly are, beyond who the world has said you are. You're able to connect with the ancient part of you that existed before you took your first breath. You're not who you thought you were – you're no longer that person – and you open the door to discovering your authentic self or who you are at soul level. The ego loses its grip, and you're invited to drop deeper into the mystical, intuitive heart.

Heart awakening can be spontaneous or gradual and it's often triggered by heartache, heartbreak, and grief. And if we find a way to keep our hearts open through the grief then we often wake up or are given the opportunity to awaken even more deeply. This can take some time and some mourning as we loosen our grip on the life that we've consciously created in order to create one that feels more true. When our heart is awakened, we're connected with our soul and are more able to connect with the souls of others. A depth of compassion, empathy, and understanding is possible when we're living with an awakened heart.

The most compassionate people I know are those who have been hurt the most, chosen to let it soften rather than harden them, and survived to live the tale. When your heart is broken and your worst fears are realized, you develop a fearlessness which, if you let it, can evoke courage. When you're there in the rubble, you get to know who you truly are from a soul perspective, beyond who others say you are. Living authentically and in congruence becomes more and more important as your ability to recognize what's in harmony and what's out of alignment is magnified.

Once the heart is opened, stretched, softened, and awake, things are different from before. The more open the heart is, the easier it is to feel and see the hearts of others. There may be a period of cleansing as we connect with the unconditional, powerful force of love and anything that's not love falls away. Some even experience a sort of bliss and peace as they enter the honeyed, ecstatic nectar of life.

## AWAKENING OF THE BODY

Increasingly, many of us are experiencing a physical awakening of the spiritual energy dormant within the body known as Kundalini Shakti. Many side effects can occur with this energy, from physical shaking to bouts of ecstatic bliss, and from physical and emotional purging to seeing spiritual visions of past lives or ancestral memories.

This stage of the spiritual awakening journey is a kind of activation of what's been asleep on the physical, and we're called into a very direct experience of the divine moving through the physical body. We may find that in our own unique way, we're able to reconnect with our sensual, ecstatic nature and have a fuller experience of life through our body's senses as Shakti moves through the body. For many people, this stage can be very healing, especially if they have been raised to see the body as anything but sacred. For some it can be subtle, but for others it's much more intense.

Throughout the awakening of the mind, the heart, and the body, great visions, intuitive downloads, and spiritual experiences keep us captivated, inspiring us to commit to the forever expansion, the constant dance between transcendence and immanence, expansion and contraction. During these stages we're in the exciting, adventurous part of our awakening journey.

Then, for some, years or even decades later, after the ascent comes the descent, as the soul is invited to incarnate even deeper. These are the dark nights of the soul. Here we're invited into the depths, descending into the soil of our cells, humanity, and the Earth. Those who cross this threshold enter an entirely new initiatory awakening phase, which we'll dive into together in the next chapter.

## SOUL INQUIRY

*Do the stages of awakening described resonate with you? If so, which of the above have you experienced (remembering that everyone's journey is unique)?*

She woke up in the middle of
her life and was astutely aware:

the dark night of the soul
was a birth canal and
she was rebirthing herself.

*rebirth* △

# △
# THE DESCENT: THE DARK NIGHTS OF THE SOUL

*'There can be no rebirth without a dark night of the soul, a total annihilation of all that you believed in and thought that you were.'*

HAZRAT INAYAT KHAN

Some glamorize the spiritual awakening process, implying that it's primarily light and love, expanding highs, unity consciousness, deep peace, ecstatic bliss, and spiritual visions. One thing's for certain: they haven't been through the dark nights of the soul. I call this phase 'the descent' as very often we find ourselves hurtling into the underworld of our body, the Earth, humanity, our ancestry, and the past.

This part of the spiritual awakening journey is where so many of us are right now. And there are not many maps to help us navigate it. It's here that we're invited to descend into what's been hidden in the shadows, inherited, pushed down, silenced, ignored, or bypassed. And not just by ourselves. We come face-to-face with the wounds that are stored deep in the cells of our bodies from our childhood, our ancestry, and the collective. And many find the Great Mother waiting for them there.

We're called to go deeper than we ever have before as we welcome more and more of our soul here, into our body, and onto the planet. And as we do, we discover the lost parts of us that demand to be held and seen. And those parts ask that we sit with them as they feel in order to heal.

For some, the descent can be sparked by the astrological transits of midlife, such as the second Saturn Return. Or by an initiation such as a loss, a death, a significant change, a global or cultural event, or a mystical experience. It can also come on more gradually as the body recovers from the expansive and energetically active stages of the ascent.

The upward expansion of those earlier stages of awakening, described in the previous chapter, create space for spirit to drop deeper into matter. And some of us are hurled deeper and deeper underground, right down to the soil and the bones of our bodies, where we begin to process personal, collective, and intergenerational trauma that until now hasn't been safe enough to feel and face.

This is the long inner winter of the spiritual journey. And it's only through surrendering to its mysterious intelligence that the buds of a brand-new spring will return. These are the excruciating, holy days of rebirth. Of transfiguration. Of dying and being reborn while still fully living. If we choose to cross this threshold, we're invited to allow our soul to come more fully into our body and the planet. This can be painful as we're forced to confront any separation or shadows that we find along the way. We must face the polarity and separation of this human life. And it takes as long as it takes, which is often much longer than we want.

In the darkness of the descent, we may feel disconnected from the warm light of the divine that we so intimately felt and knew before. We may find that the spiritual practices, teachings, and ways of living that once nourished and held us so deeply no longer work the way they did before. This doesn't mean they were wrong – it's just that we're in a different place now.

## ENTERING THE FERTILE VOID

After my mystical experience with the Great Mother, I kept being called more deeply to my body and the Earth. The Goddess came to me every night in my dreams, and I'd often wake up smelling the dark, damp soil. Black Madonnas appeared everywhere, and my home turned into a shrine to the Goddess in her many faces. The spiritual practices that had served me so well earlier in my awakening journey no longer seemed to, and I couldn't shake a sudden urge to be in nature all day long. I was also diagnosed with a chronic illness and forced to put my body first.

During this time, it felt as if much of my life started to crumble. The unrealistic pedestals on which I'd put my idols and teachers began to fall. Structures that previously seemed steady began to tremble and anything in the shadows began to emerge. Unbelievably, Craig had a mystical experience of his own a couple of weeks before mine, which completely changed him and left him questioning his own calling and purpose in life.

We both felt a deep ache to live more in harmony with nature and somewhere we could more easily afford. After more than a decade in London, we decided to move to Glastonbury, a town in southwest England where I felt my connection with the Goddess the strongest. It was unexpected but deeply led.

Little by little I connected with the Great Mother Goddess on my daily walks on the land in Glastonbury, and I started receiving downloads for the spiritual practices I needed the most. These were all centered on connecting with the sacred, intelligent pulse of the Earth, on falling into the arms of the Great Mother: from Earth pulsing to intuitive nature walking; from forest cocooning (a deeply restorative rebirthing practice I co-created with my friend Tasha Stevens) to channeling messages from the consciousness of nature, such as plants; from intuitive dance, where the body's intelligence processes stuck feelings through movement, to breathing with the trees; and from herbal tea meditations to the manifesting like a flower practice.

With each step I took and with each new feminine practice, it was as if my soul was being invited to fall deeper and deeper into the arms of the Great Mother, the Earth, humanity, and my body. I began sharing these new practices every month with my online membership community, The Sanctuary, and we practiced them together. I didn't know it at the time, but these practices would hold me and others strongly through the deepest descent of the dark nights of the soul that followed and later, would form part of The Inner Temple Mystery School Training I created.

For some of us who are experiencing the dark nights of the soul, it can feel as if we're going backward or even losing our mind, for we're feeling, purging, processing, and clearing much more than what's just our own. We're doing it on behalf of those past, present, and yet to come. It's as if the soul has an appointment – as if it chose this body, this life, at this time.

Things are different now, you're different now, the world's different now. You've been flung into the great mystery of life and the only way out is through.

The descent can be made easier if there are ones in your system who are willing to do it alongside you. Or to sit awake alongside you. To reassuringly hold your head, your heart, and your feet. But many souls come into lines and systems that are fast asleep or resistant to change. If this is you, know that if your soul chose it, you have what it takes to get through even the darkest night, after which always comes the brightest dawn. It can feel as though you're dying, metaphorically speaking, when in fact, you're deep in the long, initiatory passage of your own rebirth.

The dark nights of the soul invite our soul to come fully into our incarnation and to search for the sacred that's always been here. Our soul is hurtling ever deeper into our bodies, our ancestry, the Earth, and our humanity.

It's during the descent that soul and spirit can be woven fully into the physical in a whole different way than before. Stitched deeper. Heaven and Earth become one. The sacred and the physical merge. We learn that we can experience the divine in our bodies. We can go direct to God, for God is within every single cell. Life and death dance forever together. Spirit is planted here in the physical. And the soul is the seed for it all to happen.

The more deeply our soul descends, the higher it can ascend. Contraction, expansion, contraction, expansion. The more deeply we incarnate, the more deeply we can be here for others. All separation and pain come up to be healed. It's a passage of life in which it feels as though the connection we once had with the Spirit of Life has deserted us in a way, as we're left to sit face-to-face with all that isn't love and light.

## LEARNING TO SEE IN THE DARK

During the dark nights of the soul there's no skirting the surface. This is, after all, the descent – into the Earth, into our bodies, into our underworld. We may be given unexpected initiations in which we're brought to our knees and question all that we previously so wholeheartedly believed. We're invited to surrender to the great mystery over certainty, and our humanity is humbled in a way that's hard to describe. Our heart is stretched, and we're pummeled into returning to the Earth and humanity in a much deeper way than before.

During my descent, accompanied by the energy of dark mother Goddesses such as Demeter, Hecate, Innana, Kali, Tara, Isis, Mary Magdalene, the Black Madonna, Ishtar, and the Morrigan, I was led back to my body, my ancestry, and into the arms of nature. I learned how to see in the dark and discovered that what seemed like a tomb was actually a womb through which I'd learn to hold and birth myself.

In her 1913 book *Mysticism*, the English mystical poet Evelyn Underhill wrote about the path of awakening as a mystic's way where one can set up a direct relationship with the sacred. She recorded the five steps of living a mystical life: awakening, purification, illuminations, dark night of the soul, and union. Who we are when we enter the dark night and who we'll be when we re-emerge are not the same person. The only way through the darkest nights is to sacrifice who we once were to be born anew. It's here that we experience a metaphorical death while in the middle of our life.

*The Cloud of Unknowing,* a 14th-century spiritual text that inspired such great mystics as the Spaniard St. John of the Cross, described it like this: 'Whatever you do, this darkness and the cloud are between you and your God and hold you back from seeing him clearly by the light of understanding in your reason and from experiencing him in the sweetness of love in your feelings.'

The descent is the part of the spiritual journey we'd prefer to skip over. And it's certainly not what we signed up for when we first embarked on it or said yes to going deeper. I wonder if this is the part when the mystics of old would pack it all in and head to a cave in the wilderness. Did they do that just to be in union with the beloved or did they also do it to process their dark nights away from society and the innocent bystanders who would have to witness the tumultuous purging and purification that goes with it?

The deepest depths of my descent occurred when I had a newborn in tow, so my mystical-cave-exit from society was postponed and done instead in between the busy messiness of my everyday life. Maybe yours was, too? I've observed in others going through the darkest nights the same deep urge to be in nature that I experienced. An urge to return to the Earth. To our bodies. To our humanity. To our ancestry. To return to the wilderness and to the arms of the Mother/Sacred Feminine, who's been absent for so long.

Cloaked in the darkest nights, seemingly separated from the divine we once so deeply knew, we're invited to search for heaven in the seed and the cell, the flowers, the waters, the trees. In our loved ones, ourselves, and our enemies too. It was in nature that I felt the most peace and began to see God where I previously had not: in the flowers, the stones, the waters, the plants, and the trees. In the mountains, the seasons, and in all of Life. Was this because as a species we've become disconnected from nature and thus the Spirit of Life? And does the descent reconnect us with it? Is this happening as part of humanity's survival on Earth, inviting us to return to and protect our home? Or is it part of our spiritual evolution, regardless of the state of the planet we find ourselves in and on?

I believe that so many of us have been going through a collective dark night of the soul. And while this part of the spiritual journey has been documented by the mystics, sages, shamans, medicine people, and saints of old, we're living in a different time now. One of great change, urgency, and awakening.

Perhaps what makes the time in which we're living unique is that we are collectively having to learn how to navigate so many complex issues at the same time, including global warming, war, genocide, ecocide, colonialism, capitalism, patriarchy, a deeper understanding of intergenerational trauma – which seems to be coming up to be healed collectively – and increased life expectancy, amongst other things.

As a society we try to avoid change and the potent teachers of winter and autumn (fall), of death and aging; we've forgotten the great wisdom that these sacred portals impart and thus remain asleep. But if we find a way back to the teachings of nature, we'll find the most ancient mystery school waiting there. It will show us how Life is always trying to initiate us into becoming even more of ourselves. And we'll discover that the darkness is not only the end, but also the beginning. And if we embrace it and the great mystery, one day soon we'll be rebirthed.

## REBIRTH: THE RETURNING

Many mystics speak of a stage after the dark nights of the soul where we experience an intimate merging with the beloved as we return from the underworld completely changed. After what feels like an eternity in the dark, our soul re-emerges transformed. It's hard to put our finger on it – we know that no part of us is who we were and yet somehow, we're more ourselves than ever before. The dark nights have taught us how to see in the dark and that it's actually in the darkness that all of life is reborn. Our worst fears have been realized and we've survived. This gives us a grounded, unshakable strength, faith, and holding that no one can take from us.

And while in some ways it feels that we're back where we were, that we've returned, nothing could be further from the truth, for we're not the same person and the only journey we made was deep within. We discover that the dark nights were actually the womb in which we rebirthed ourselves. There's a humbling that the dark nights bring. Once we're brought to our knees, belly to the earth, temple in the heart, we find a home that can never be taken from us. And from this steady soil, we can drop our roots deeper and our hearts wider than before.

Rebirth isn't possible without complete surrender to the unknown. We must sacrifice who we were and our understanding of the world to be reborn in the middle of our lives.

And sacred embodiment isn't possible without the descent – as we descend into our bodies, to each other (humanity), and back to the garden of the Earth, we integrate all we've learned at different stages of our spiritual journey. Perhaps, the deeper we descend into the physical, the higher we can soar in the spiritual. Maybe the whole point of the awakening journey is to bring spirit into matter, light into form; maybe the whole point of the dark nights of the soul is to embody it all.

We're living in times between times. Rebirthing times. Transfiguration times. A collective dark night of the soul. Perhaps what feels like a death could actually be our individual and collective rebirth.

## SOUL INQUIRY

*Have you ever been through the dark nights of the soul? If so, how did it change you?*

*If you're in it right now, how is it changing you?*

# the
## descent

The purification wasn't pretty.
It made her and those around her who
hadn't been through it
think she was going backward, when she wasn't.
It didn't look enlightened,
but the purging was indeed lightening
something more ancient within her.

The heaviness that existed before she did.
The very thing her soul came here to clear.
Freeing her of the density, rage, and grief of all
that had been left unspoken by those of the past.
From times where it wasn't safe to do so.
The same density that keeps us stuck and asleep.

If she had been born in a different age,
in a different land,
she would be revered for what
her soul had the courage to do.
But in these times, it was still
misdiagnosed and misunderstood.

Only those who had been through
their own dark nights knew how
to sit alongside her.

An initiate knows an initiate when they see one,
and that no one can return from the underworld
without first facing the demons within.
But when they re-emerge, they won't
only have rebirthed themselves.
Their presence will also have the potential to birth
something within someone else.

△

# LET IT CRUMBLE, LET IT FALL

The end is also the beginning. The crumbling happens so you can find your ground. The falling happens so you can see a new way through the trees. The shedding happens so you have room to expand and grow. If the crumbling, the falling, and the shedding don't happen, things will stagnate, suffocate, and rot, and then nothing new can grow.

You've probably felt the winds shifting for a while. Maybe at first, they were gentle enough to ignore, but now, no more. This time of transition, these changing, unpredictable winds, you can sense them in the cloak of night when the rest of the world is asleep.

Fear not that the tides are turning, for there's a new current coming in. It's designed to take you out to sea and transport you to new shores. But first you must dive into these uncharted waters and let them carry you. The longer you fight them, the more exhausted you'll get. For the direction of travel was chosen before you took your first breath. Keep your heart to the heavens and your arms open wide. The sooner you do this, the sooner you'll discover that Life is actually on your side.

I know it's scary – navigating changing times like these always is. But by now, you have enough experience to recognize that this is a pivotal part of your path. The souls here now on Earth are changing at a rapid rate. After being dormant for millennia, they're being urged to wake up and clear the ancestral lines.

The souls who are awake and here right now are the ones to do it on behalf of those who came before them and those yet to come. They contributed to all of this too, in ways that you cannot quite make out. I know that right now clinging on seems like the most comforting thing to do. But don't you remember that you came here to birth this world anew?

So come dreamers, come cycle breakers, come courageous ones, come mighty of heart. Let's gather and stay true to what we chose at the very start.

## SOUL INQUIRY

*What is crumbling or falling away?*

The parts of her that were dying
clung on for dear life.
They were not about to go quietly.
They urged her not to forget the
good times they'd had.

And the times they'd protected her so fiercely.
How she would not be who or where
she was without them.
And they were right.

She laid rose petals at their feet.
They softened and shared that they
were afraid of the great unknown.
And also excited about the great unknown
they were about to meet.

*parts of us are always dying* △

Δ

# HOW IS LIFE TRYING
# TO INITIATE YOU?

It's the extremes of life that initiate us the most. And these are extreme times. Life is always trying to initiate us into becoming even more of who we truly are. As individuals, as humans, as a planet. Right now, how is Life trying to initiate you?

In times of solitude, we're called to go inward. In times of upheaval, we're called to loosen our grip on that which is no longer aligned. In times of heartbreak, we're called to find a way to let it crack us open. In all times we're called to connect with our true inner nature and the interconnected true nature of all of Life.

It's in extreme times like these that the things which aren't sustainable become clear. Where if we go in, we're able to see our lives in a different light. To see all that doesn't matter. To see all that we've taken for granted. To see that being alive on this planet is a great privilege.

Life is always trying to initiate us, and deep inside we know that the only way to surrender to the initiation is to surrender to the innate power and great mystery within. This power is internal, but it's also connected with the intelligence that exists within all Life. It's the same energy that tells flowers when to bloom and it was present when you grew in the womb. Trust in that. It will carry you through.

Embrace the certain death of the past. Surrender to what's wanting to be born through you. Life is always trying to initiate us into becoming even more of who we truly are – you can resist it or embrace it, but Life will continue to do what it knows how to do. So many of us fear change, yet change is the most certain thing in the world.

> **To be initiated means to cross a threshold,**
> **to go from one state of being to another.**
> **Often, it requires a period of uncertainty.**

We cannot go back to the way things were, but it's not yet clear how things will be. And so, our only choice is to walk through the fire of the unknown. We head into the abyss in order to journey back into the world changed. As we cross the threshold it's clear that things will never be the same again. We're asked to walk blindly into a whole new world and a whole new way of being. Forever changed. Life is always trying to initiate us, but few people accept the invitation for the initiation.

There comes a time when the flower knows that it can no longer remain in the protective constraints of the bud. Somehow, it needs to trust in the birthing energy which is encoded within Life and surrender to the unknown of the future bloom.

The same birthing energy exists within all of nature and in birth, both literal and metaphorical. There are rolling contractions as the souls prepare to make their entrance into this world. As we transition from one thing to another we're called to burst through the constraints of the seed and then the certainty of the bud, so that something new can bloom. And once the bloom is here, we'll be called to face another initiation as our petals give way to the fruit that will follow, if we allow it.

## SOUL INQUIRY

*Right now, how is Life trying to initiate you?*

I can feel myself beckoning me forth,
from a place of not yet.
Leaving clues of my becoming,
that I can sense but not quite yet see.

A choir of future selves sings me on.
Timeless notes sent one by one,
from me, for me.

They fill the ineffable chambers
of my heart, which words cannot.

*becoming* △

## △
# REBIRTHED

In the weeks and months after my mystical experience in the center of the Earth with the Cosmic Mother, I could still feel it deep in my heart. The potency of the pure sweet energy was like honey running through my system. I didn't tell many people about the experience – it had been so deeply intimate that I wanted to keep it close and stabilize the energy before sharing it with the world.

At night the Shakti energy continued to work through me, resulting in spontaneous shaking in my body. Years earlier, in 2012, I'd experienced another Shakti awakening over a period of about nine months. However, what I've learned about Kundalini Shakti awakenings is that each one is very intimate and completely unique, delivering whatever is most needed by the individual. And while this awakening of the body is completely natural and in other cultures would be received with deep support and reverence, in my culture not much was or is known about it, so it was quite a lonely thing to go through.

The energy seemed to have an intelligence to it, and it was unquestionably physical. In the first Kundalini Shakti awakening period in 2012 it felt like a very clear upward spiraling of ecstatic energy. However, from 2017 onward, as I entered the descent, the energy was clearing things from my cells and joints, as well as trauma from childhood and this life, inherited through my cells from my ancestry and from the collective.

Anything that hadn't been felt needed to be felt, in order to clear it. It was as if, through my mystical experience, more of my soul, spirit, and universal energy had entered and expanded within my body, and as it did, it woke anything that was unlike it from within my body to be healed. Any moment of separation was to be felt – grief, hurt, rage, shame, repressed memories, unprocessed feelings, and trauma – my own, inherited, and collective.

It was as if the first Kundalini Shakti awakening had been about reconnecting with the Spirit of Life, with the intelligent, ecstatic pulse of Life. And now, in 2017, this deep descent, these dark nights of the soul, were showing me all the separation that I'd experienced in the physical. Expansion and contraction. The opposites. The polarity of the soul's journey on this planet with an invitation to marry the two – spirit and matter, transcendence and immanence, heaven and Earth.

One night some months after my mystical experience with the Great Mother, the Shakti energy began moving through me as I lay beside Craig in bed, and I entered another spontaneous trance state. Eyes closed, I found myself trapped inside a dark tunnel, unable to get out. It took a few minutes, but then I realized that the tunnel was the birth canal. Once again, I was being shown the gates of Life – this time, through re-experiencing my own birth 36 years earlier!

I felt the intensity of the contractions as I moved through my mother's body, and then I hurtled from the watery world of her womb, where all my needs were met, into this world. Startled, I took in my first breath. And with this first breath I was suddenly overwhelmed by a feeling from head to toe that something was terribly wrong. And that feeling turned into a belief that there was something wrong with *me*. Where did this thought come from? Was it of the body or the soul?

I experienced the moment of separation from my first love, my mother. It felt like a fall from Grace, an unshakable grief that still existed within me. I wondered, do we all still have the grief from that first moment of separation, deep down? I saw how birth is a huge initiation for the soul – going from union to separation, from spirit to matter, to truly descend and incarnate. I wondered, is there a way not to feel the grief of this separation? Or is this part of the soul's descent, the soul's incarnation into a body on Earth?

I was shown how this early experience and others that followed were deeply imprinted in my cells and that they had informed my entire life. I was shown how this blueprint is passed down at a cellular level through our ancestral lines. How trauma, fear, belief, and shame are held in the cells and passed down this way too, and how at this time we're being called to heal on behalf of those who could not.

I saw how this belief that there was something wrong with me or that I'd done something wrong even before I'd taken my first breath had been driving me throughout my life. It had led to working myself into utter exhaustion in a never-ending bid to be independent and not rely on others, and to trying to receive love and approval through doing, rather than knowing it innately and simply being.

I saw how this separation I experienced – and perhaps you've experienced something similar, too – stops us from knowing the holy innocence that's our birthright. I saw how this belief that I'd done something wrong and that there was something wrong with me had led to unhealthy methods of survival which later resulted in a chronic autoimmune illness and other health conditions that were driven by a nervous system that constantly scanned for potential threats and danger.

It had resulted in a fear of sharing my voice and it explained why I was finding it so difficult to be 'out and visible' in the world publicly as my work spread more widely. I was then shown how these conditions were also the crucible in which my creative gifts and sensitivities were consecrated. And while all this wasn't serving me in current times, I wondered, did my soul actually choose it?

Years later, while I was nursing my newborn son, my mother shared a previously missing piece of information that helped me understand this mystical experience on a deeper level. On the day of my birth, she explained, there had been more newborn babies than available beds in the hospital and after spending a few hours in a corridor, Mum and I were put in a room with a mother whose baby had just died. Grief and celebration, birth and death, life and tragedy, congratulations and condolences, all in one space. The sounds of a suckling baby combined with the sobs of a mother mourning her child.

The last time my mum had given birth she was a teenager, after being sent away to a Catholic convent to give up her baby for adoption. And now, 10 years later, there I was in her arms, and beside her, a mother without her child. My mum said she felt guilty about her good fortune and my health and that she tried to keep me quiet so as not to distress the grieving mother even more.

When my mum told me this story I began to cry. For that woman who'd had to endure the worst pain possible when she should have been experiencing the exact opposite. For the brutal extremes of this human life. I wondered how this birth experience had informed me. Could these first moments and days of my life have created a blueprint within me, influencing the trajectory of my life?

I wondered whether my fascination with death and dying from a young age was due to that. Was it why, at the tender age of 14, I'd taken a bus to the library to borrow Elisabeth Kübler-Ross's *On Death and Dying* instead of the book my friends were reading, Ann M. Martin's *The Baby-Sitter's Club*? Was this why I'd found myself spontaneously crossing paths with and developing relationships with women who had lost their children and channeling messages from them? And why as a teenager, I would sit with them for hours and just listen?

Was this why I was so drawn to grief and the depths of the human experience? And why I kept experiencing the two gates of Life – birth and death – together? Are our first experiences imprinted on our cells and do they inform our lives from there? Does the soul choose it? These are the mysteries that captivate my mind and heart.

## SOUL INQUIRY

*Have you been told the story of your birth?*

*If it's possible, ask your mother or anyone else who might know about your birth to tell you your birth story.*

*If your biological mother is no longer alive, isn't present in your life, or you don't have the kind of relationship where this conversation is possible, is there anyone else you can ask for more information about your birth? If you were adopted, is there anywhere you can go, online or in person, to look for more information about your birth?*

# △
# GREAT MOTHER AWAKENING

The Great Mother is stirring within the hearts and cells of many. She's urging us to wake up, in the middle of our lives, to ourselves and to each other. She's in every cry, longing, and yearning. She's beneath it all. In our pain and sorrow and in our joy, too. Urging us to remember how intrinsically connected we all are.

From soul to seed, tree to cell. Anything that's living is not separate from you. Your sorrow is the evidence of how much you love and how much you long for connection. Your sorrow is born from your connection. If you weren't connected you wouldn't feel the longing or the pain, for your heart would be closed over.

We've gotten it wrong – seeing those who dream and long and feel and dive to the depths and experience the divine directly as not strong. But the tender-hearted and open-minded are not weak. The tender-hearted and open-minded are the most courageous of us all. They're the ones who dare, even amid all this separation, to say, there is another way. And this other way will save us.

Somewhere along the way, the Goddess was banished and buried, the Divine Feminine within us all forced to go underground. But now, the Great Mother is stirring and urging us to awaken and mend what's been broken. To process the pain. To be part of the reimagining and rebirthing of our species before it's too late – for us, not for Her.

*Let the stirring within your heart wake you from your slumber. Let it hurl you from your numbness. Let it show you how to truly live.*

After my mystical experience in 2017, I started having several recurring dreams that made me sense that the Great Mother was awakening something deep within my heart and cells. Each night I'd find myself in a different ancient European square with a giant stone statue of a male God towering above me – it was so tall that I couldn't even make out his face. The square itself was empty, barren. Life-force was absent. The Goddess was nowhere to be seen.

Then, suddenly, there was a rumble inside the Earth, and the male God statue came crashing down to my feet. Through the cracks in the hard, broken stone, two young girls arose from the dark fertile soil beneath. Two turned into three, then 30, 300, 3,000. The girls grew into Goddesses. Embodiments of the divine. Goddesses everywhere the eye could see. Innocent. Abundant. Unrestrained. Wild. Sensual. Free.

The Divine Feminine had returned in a way different from before and there was no stopping Her. The wildflowers and the weeds followed, and they also couldn't be contained or cut back. Ivy took over those ancient squares, becoming so abundant that there was no stone to be seen, and they now resembled the wild garden of the Earth. A virgin forest. Embodied Eden. Nature had reclaimed what was originally hers. Then, right on cue, I'd wake up, smelling the fertile, abundant, damp, feminine Earth.

If we track back through our ancestral lines, we'll find something in common: worship of the Earth as the Sacred Feminine, Goddess, or Mother. And that makes sense because each of us grew inside a mother, regardless of whether they were who raised us. Their body was the portal through which we came to life. Moving from their waters into the waters of this world. You need only see the way a baby looks to their mother to know this is true. To them, the mother is Life, Goddess, Creator of it all!

The annihilation of the feminine as sacred may have begun with the mass slaughter of the Indigenous tribes of ancient Europe by the Roman Empire. And continued with the persecution of the wisdom keepers and wise women and Earth-worshiping tribes of the Middle Ages, when it was forbidden to honor and work with and worship the Goddess, nature, and the Earth as holy. Centuries later came colonialism, patriarchy, and toxic capitalism and all the tragic harm that they inflicted in all corners of the world.

This loss of the feminine as sacred saw us evolve from tribal, cyclic living in reverence to nature and the seasons to, eventually, overly individualized civilizations focused on separation and greed, with land becoming a resource to conquer and own rather than something precious to protect and revere.

> *I believe that the Great Mother in her*
> *many different faces is coming to us all.*
> *She's urging us to heal what's been*
> *severed deep in our cells.*

She's saying that each one of us should play a role in the healing of humanity. And that she's available to guide us, right here and right now. But to heal what's been severed, we must feel. And right now, the Great Mother is waking us in the many to find the courage to do so. The process isn't pretty. It's largely misunderstood. And many feel as if they're doing this work alone. If this is you, know that while you may be alone in your immediate life, you're not alone in doing this work. And the Great Mother and the Ancient Grandmothers of your lineages are singing you on.

Perhaps your soul chose to be here, in this body, at this time, in these ancestral lines. Make no mistake, this time isn't easy, but it is important. You're here because your soul chose it. At a soul level, we all dreamed of this time. Trust in the intelligence of your cells. They're part of the great intelligent Spirit of Life. Trust in the call of your soul. It too is part of the great intelligence of Life.

A great transmutation is happening within your body and the body of humanity and the Earth. These are the times that follow on from the great awakening.

Decades of integration and rebirth. Integration isn't easy, but it is necessary. Rebirth isn't possible without it. And you're holding a thread for the healing of humanity. Trust the thread you are holding.

## SOUL INQUIRY

*What is the Great Mother awakening within your heart?*

Anchor your soul in your body,
so you can withstand the coming winds.

If you see 'God,' the divine, the sacred as
anywhere but within you, everything has
the potential to knock you over.

But if you find your holiness in your wholeness,
in your Earthiness, in your humanness,
nothing can knock you off course, for you know
that the sacred is rooted deep within.

*unshakable* △

△

# KEEPING YOUR HEART
# SOFT AND OPEN

One of Life's biggest challenges is keeping your heart open through the extremes. No one is immune to the highs and lows of the human experience. From the ecstasy to the agony, the joy to the grief, the love to the loss. If we truly want to experience the bliss, we can't bypass the difficult parts of being human. And if you close off your heart to the grief, you won't be able to fully experience the joy.

Flowers teach us this, season after season. They know that if they don't surrender to fall and winter, come spring and summer they won't be able to bud and bloom. Birth teaches us this too. The safer the mother feels, through the contractions, the more comfortable and confident she is to say yes to life and open.

Living with your heart open is truly a courageous act. If you can die with your heart soft and open, you've truly lived. This above all else will be your greatest triumph. When we're going through difficult times, when we most want to separate, the healing we seek is often found in connection not separation. When we close our hearts and shut down because the pain is too much, we often find we're more separate than before.

This is a time of great change and transformation. But not in the way that we might think. Threads are being woven and our hearts are being broken open. And they should be. This is what it is to live a mystical life. One where the heart is the main intelligence center, tapped into a force greater than anything our brain could ever create.

*Stay grounded on your journey and tend your aching heart. Don't close it over. Focus all on that and everything else will be taken care of.*

What's been happening since the Goddess went underground must stop. The Divine Feminine must continue to rise and return if we're to find our way back to ourselves and each other. We must go from his story and her story and birth together a new story if we're to stop reliving the same stories. One by one we're feeling what's been frozen in our ancestry. One by one, we're unearthing the actions done in separation and desperation. One by one, we're finding our way back to ourselves and each other.

Maybe the reason we've been greedy is because we were hungry for a love that we couldn't find. Our hunger for more was insatiable, no matter what we reached for. And so, we consumed and grabbed, just like we were taught to. These generations that are here and those yet to come are part of the great change. It's something we're not used to, being part of a system that's much bigger than us. There's been so much focus on individualism.

The years around 2020 roused us all from a numb slumber and brought us face-to-face with the undercurrent of humanity and society. We're still processing that. For many, what had been buried, frozen, and silenced began to thaw. We began to see beneath the surface to what was really there. That which was unable to be felt previously began to melt to be felt. That which was unable to be seen previously began to melt to be felt. That which hadn't yet been fully spoken collectively began to be expressed.

It was a much-needed reckoning on many levels, and it continues. We're still being called to soften and be broken open. We've begun to see the human where previously we saw the other. But the process of doing so and getting there has had to be seeing the separation first. For if you don't acknowledge what's broken, you can never fully heal. And to heal is to make whole.

Humanity is whole, part of a larger whole. However, without the acknowledgment of the separation and the pain that's come from this separation, we'll never truly heal. Individually or collectively. Until we see all as part of a larger whole, our path will become more difficult. For we're not tapping into the energy of the whole, of the Spirit of Life. And life wants to support life.

All the healing you do contributes to the whole. All the healing done by the whole can be felt by the individual. Learn to see all those who are struggling as in pain. Learn to see yourself as a precious child of the Goddess. We all are. It's no accident that you're here at this time. Remember why you chose to come.

## SOUL INQUIRY

*Who are you being called to soften your heart toward?*

*How can you soften your heart toward yourself?*

# △
# THE BIRTH MYSTERIES

One of the most potent ways that the Great Mother continued to deliver her teachings to me during this time was through pregnancy, childbirth, and loss. I didn't expect it, but this period of my life would go on to teach me more than any other.

As my body knitted soul into form through my pregnancies and I approached the gates of Life through birth and the loss of a baby, I noticed that I was physically experiencing so many of the spiritual and mystical principles and teachings I'd learned over the previous two decades in the ascent stage of my spiritual awakening. In this chapter, I share a little about this period of my life and some of the insights it brought me. If pregnancy, birth, or baby loss are difficult topics for you, please feel free to skip ahead to the next chapter.

During my twenties and early thirties, I wasn't fully sure if I wanted to have children. I had a deep fear that becoming a mother would stop me from being able to do the work I came here to do. None of the mystics I'd read about had children, and I was concerned that I'd struggle to find the space, quiet, and energy to create art.

However, over time, something changed, and during a pilgrimage to the ancient temples of Egypt, as I lay in a secret chamber in the temple complex at Dendera devoted to the Goddess Hathor, I heard the words 'Your body is a portal; birth is a portal for souls to enter the Earth,' and became aware of a golden presence that I sensed might be my future child. When we returned from Egypt to our little cottage in Glastonbury, I discovered I was pregnant.

As a mystic who had studied the journey of the soul with an insatiable vigor, I was excited to experience the soul's incarnation and journey through the gates of Life in such a physical way. Each of my three pregnancies taught me something unique and changed me physically, mentally, emotionally, and spiritually.

## TRUSTING THE BODY'S ANCIENT INTELLIGENCE

My first pregnancy was a deeply healing initiatory time in which I not only prepared for motherhood but dove deep into my own personal healing. As my son grew within me, his presence activated an intense ancient feminine power that I'd never accessed before. If this pregnancy taught me anything it was to trust the intelligence of my body over any external source.

At this point, I want to acknowledge that I realize how privileged I am to have access to healthcare and grateful to have had choices that many women do not. But despite all of this, the health professionals' insistence that the path they were laying out was the only way forward didn't feel true to me. From deep within me erupted this fierce ancient feminine warrior who screamed that there was nothing wrong with me or my baby.

I was shown how to trust the ancient feminine wisdom of my body in a medical system that did not revere it and experienced an initiatory fire and power within me that demanded that I stand up for myself in a way I never had previously. I saw how the way our culture sees and treats birth is a metaphor for our relationship with life in general. I saw how disconnected we've become from the intelligence of nature and how we attempt to control every aspect of it, believing we're above it and know better, rather than being part of it.

I gave birth to my son at home – in a pool in the center of our living room – a privilege for which I'd fought extremely hard. My waters didn't break, and he was born en caul, still in his amniotic sac. The birth was empowering, fast, and excruciating, and the energy was intense, ancient, and deep. Sunny came blasting into this world like a meteorite hitting the Earth.

Just before I transitioned, I experienced reaching the gates of Life, just as I had during my mystical experience with the Great Cosmic Mother in 2017. Everything got really still, and I felt the tides shift and the portal open, just as they had in the Egyptian temple, and I knew my son was ready to come.

I felt connected to all the women in my ancestral line and felt them roaring with me and through me. It was the most transcendent and immanent, physical and mystical experience of my life, all at once. In birthing Sunny I tapped into a cellular inner power that I never knew I had. Everything changed within me that day.

## ONE MINUTE LIFE, THE NEXT DEATH

Just after Sunny's second birthday we discovered we were pregnant again. While visiting family in Australia at the tail end of the COVID-19 lockdowns, I woke on Christmas morning and discovered I was bleeding.

With doctors' offices closed and hospitals on limited operation, it took two days to confirm what I already knew – we'd lost the baby. I was informed of this while being examined alone at the hospital; Craig wasn't allowed to enter the building. Afterward, I found him sitting on the grass outside and I didn't have to say anything. We sat there frozen in silence, and my eyes fixated on a teeny white feather at my feet, pure as snow.

Time slowed down and as we drove back home, I noticed that familiar feeling, the one where you can't understand how everything and everyone is going on as normal when your world's been torn apart. I'd experienced an early miscarriage years before. This loss came later in the pregnancy and the following days were excruciating. I was surprised by the visceral, physical pain, much like my full-term birth, with contractions and all.

The grief was guttural and raw, and it hit us in different ways. For me it was emotional and physical. I couldn't stop thinking about the fact that one moment I'd had life within me, and everything was so full of hope, and then the next, there was death and such deep sorrow. I wondered, at what point does life turn to death and what's the difference. Does the soul change its mind, or did it always only ever want to be here for that length of time?

I threw myself into my writing and work, which helped me wade through the longing and grief. One day while walking along the Sydney waterfront, I received an outline for the structure of The Inner Temple Mystery School, which would become my foundational training. I'd received the initial download and vision for this training during my kirtan teacher training years earlier, but I hadn't been able to land the mystery school's form until this moment.

A surge of creative energy took over me and together, Craig and I established the foundations of the mystery school; we also hired my long-term friend Amy Firth to join us in this endeavor. I wondered if the creative life-force birthing energy that my body had planned to use to create our daughter was now being redirected into the school. Strangely, I felt her alongside us every step of the way.

Every day I'd meditate to the same song, the 'Lost Words Blessing,' playing it on repeat; it was a song like no other I'd heard before and it softened my heart in a way that's hard to describe. It felt as though it held and touched the hope and the grief within me, together. The grief of my lost baby and the hope that she'd return. The grief of the lost wisdom teachings of my ancestry and the hope to reconnect with them. The grief of the separation of the Earth as our mother and the hope to reweave the sacred thread.

Around the same time, Craig found an early 20th-century book which he said felt connected to what we were bringing in with The Inner Temple Mystery School Training and the ancient ways of our shared ancestry (Scottish and Irish). I'd planned to read the book but hadn't found the time; called *Carmina Gadelica*, it was a compilation of ancient Gaelic poems, prayers, incantations, and charms collected orally in Scotland and translated into English by Alexander Carmichael.

Many months passed and we completed the training. At one point I was invited to a dinner with my publisher, at which we were all to read a poem. Instead, I chose the lyrics of the 'Lost Words Blessing.' I began researching its origins, and I couldn't believe what I discovered. In 2010, the editors of the *Oxford Junior Dictionary* had dropped around 50 words associated with nature because they deemed them irrelevant to children these days. Words like nettle, dandelion, otter, raven, and oak were replaced by chatroom, broadband, and celebrity, among others.

Several singer-songwriters gathered and wrote the 'Lost Words Blessing' in protest at this move. The musicians said that the song had been 'inspired by blessings in Scottish Gaelic, particularly from a beautiful collection of charms and incantations called *Carmina Gadelica*.' Craig and I had both been led to the same source in our own ways. It felt deeply destined and as though our ancient ancestors were singing us on.

## SAVORING THE SWEETNESS

A few months later I became pregnant again, with my daughter Goldie. I got chills when I discovered that her due date was 25 December – the same day we'd lost the baby a year earlier. I wondered, was this a sign that her soul had returned?

The pregnancy went much more smoothly than my first, and I felt far less scared about the birth. By then I'd done so much mother line, ancestral, somatic, and nervous system healing and my wish was to give birth to her with a regulated nervous system.

During the pregnancy I started experiencing physically how different each soul is. Goldie's energy was so different to Sunny's. And it was as if she was teaching me very different things as she came into form. Her lesson to me was to remember to savor the sweetness of life. I started seeing my tendency to work hard and reward myself at the end rather than experience the joy and sweetness of life right here right now. A very capitalistic, patriarchal way of being.

The labor taught me this as well. It was so much longer than Sunny's, but a lot gentler most of the time. And so, right in the middle of the labor, I created an offering to the fire. I vowed to welcome the sweetness of life here and now, to find the beauty in every moment, to welcome joy first, without waver.

She arrived in the water of the birth pool in my living room. Slowly and gently, I brought her to the surface and watched as she took her first breath. She didn't cry and looked into my eyes so calmly, deeply, and sweetly. I held her in my arms and fully savored the moments as my heart stretched wide open and I drank in the sweetness of this life in all its extremes. So grateful for what she'd already taught me and the medicine she'd brought me.

# △
# IS THIS THE ORIGINAL WOUND?

My first pregnancy stretched me wider than I ever thought possible, in more ways than one. And it almost destroyed me. But creation cannot exist without death. It wasn't the physicalness, although Goddess knows that was intense, it was my heart.

In those first days postpartum, my friend Binnie Dansby, my wise and fabulous soul friend in her eighties, came to stay and every time I entered the room, she'd announce: 'Here comes the Goddess!' At first, I squirmed at this and laughed if off – me, with my unwashed hair, cracked nipples, and a fragile nervous system that was constantly on high alert. But then I saw my son. Like *really* saw him. The soul who had arrived. I saw the way he looked at me and my cells remembered feeling that way as a baby myself.

And I understood that Binnie was right. To him, I was THE Goddess. Creator. Bringer of Life. And in that moment, I was a goner. For how on earth could I receive all the love that he was directing toward me? It couldn't be humanly possible to hold that amount of love in one human heart. It made me think, if he came in with that amount of love, then maybe I did too. Maybe we all did.

Were our mothers able to receive that amount of love, too? Is any mother able to fully receive it if they weren't received that way themselves? To witness the soul who has arrived Earth-side and the immense journey they have undertaken to be here, in this body, on this planet, at this time. To receive the gallons of love that they come in with. Is this the original wound?

And then love does what it knows how to do best – it brings up everything that's unlike it. And each time it does, we get to decide whether to put it in a box and throw away the key or keep our hearts open and let the love of the world blast through us. The first is easier – it's what we're taught to do. The latter will rip you to smithereens. But if you let it break you, it will also remake you. And that's rebirth.

Suddenly, I was much more deeply invested in truly being here. I hadn't realized it at the time, but prior to Sunny's birth I'd had one foot in and one foot out. Now that there was someone I was here to protect, though, I was way more attached to the outcome. My heart swung from extreme, blissful love to unimaginable loss in the same breath. The protective roar of all the mothers grew louder within me. And with that came sacred rage and sobering grief.

*A child comes in with a portal of love in their heart that's so vast, connected, and potent that it has the capacity to heal the wounds of the world. If we let it.*

Perhaps our capacity to recognize, witness, receive, and validate the love that every child comes in with is the most healing work of all. Witnessing this in another is the greatest gift we can give. This simple yet complex act has the power to heal not just them and you but the entire world.

Our society is set up in the wrong way. We see children as lesser beings to whom we can teach our ways. But what if we saw them as the great teaches and healers that they are? Children are designed to stretch our hearts open and sometimes this means that we feel broken. What if parents were given the support that they need to properly receive the ones who come? And to process the times when they themselves were not. What if we looked at our elders in that way too? What if those who are the closest to the breath of angels and the gates of Life were seen as the ones who know best? What if the nearer someone is to birth and death, the more we revere their wisdom and insight? The world would be a very different place.

Could this be one of the invitations from Life? To have our hearts stretched so fully open that we can hold the whole world and all the children of this planet in there, too?

## SOUL INQUIRY

*When did you start closing your heart off to the world?*

*What does the child within you need to hear today?*

△

# ANCIENT FEMININE GRIEF, POWER, AND RAGE

During the final moments of my son's birth, I experienced traveling through my maternal line all the way back to the Original Mother and being connected to the power and rage and grief of all the women who had ever stood at the gates of Life and returned. I felt them screaming with me and through me. I saw the layers of protection around my cells exploding like bombs, scattering to the ends of the cosmos. And then I was hurled deep into the center point of my body as Sunny arrived.

I felt a ferocious love for him, one that I hadn't known was possible. And at the same time, I felt such fear and grief at the thought of ever losing him. I was incredibly grateful to be his mother yet also deeply worried about the world that he'd inherit. I felt a strong urge to do anything for him, even while my body was hurting as it knitted itself back together after giving birth.

I was prepared for the sleepless nights and the hard work of mothering, but not for the transformation that being present to that depth of love would do to my heart, which felt raw and wide open. Nor for how deeply I'd be called into the work of healing the ancestral mother line. I didn't realize how sensitive I'd feel at a cellular level. My son's entrance into the world sent me deeper into my Great Mother awakening, too, as I noticed how much more connected I felt to all the children of the Earth. Do all mothers feel like this?

Postpartum is a sensitive phase in normal times, but it was clear that these were not normal times. The world was going through its own dark nights of the soul. On several continents, wildfires roared; everything and everyone was locked down during the COVID-19 pandemic; divisiveness and cancel culture grew rampant, and a much-needed racial reckoning arose. Deep awakening, separation, trauma processing, and healing were the backdrop to my postpartum months.

It seemed as if my body was attempting to purge and process any trauma that had lain dormant within my cells. One early experience that I processed during this time was a treatment for bedwetting I'd undergone, on and off, between the ages of seven and 17; navigating this condition as a child and teen had been very difficult, and my parents had tried all kinds of methods to help me manage it.

The treatment consisted of a cold rubber and metal mat beneath my bedsheet which was hooked up to an alarm system that would activate whenever I wet the bed. Most nights, the whole bed would vibrate, and the alarm would go off like a fire truck inside my room, waking up the entire house and I'm sure the neighbors, too.

Given what we know today about the negative impact that trauma and dysregulation of the nervous system have on our health, I realize how significant a role this treatment played in my subsequent problems with sleep, anxiety, depression, and other nervous system-related issues and how it led to a later diagnosis of complex post-traumatic stress disorder (CPTSD).

Any parent of a newborn will tell you how tough it can be to deal with endless nights of broken sleep. In the early months, it's not unusual to be woken every 20 minutes by your baby crying – hello, cluster-feeding nights and cracked nipples. However, I noticed that my response to this experience seemed to be much more intense than it was for many others. Every time I was awoken by my son's cries, my whole body would immediately enter a state of emergency. I'd jump out of bed in a panic, thinking there was something terribly wrong, just as I had as a child each time the alarm system on my bed was activated.

This is just one example of the trauma that was re-triggered for me around this time; it was as if something had been unlocked and it was inviting me to clear unprocessed emotions held deep within my body. I did serious work on processing these and at the same time it felt as though the birth of my son also opened a portal for healing beyond my own trauma.

Each night, my body became white-hot and began to shake. Unprocessed emotions and intergenerational and collective trauma seemed to blast through me like a bullet train. It was extremely disorientating, confusing, and terrifying. The ancient feminine power, grief, and rage that I'd tapped into during Sunny's birth seemed to have been re-activated and it was trying to process itself through me. I felt an energy like that of the powerful Dark Feminine goddesses I'd studied during my mystical training present through me as the Shakti once again started moving through my body so physically.

In the background to this, my home country of Australia had closed its borders due to the pandemic, and so my family, who had intended to visit and support me in my first year of motherhood, couldn't get to me to help. What I didn't know then was that my dad, brother, and sister would be unable to meet my son or see me as a mother until he was two years old. Those baby years, gone.

Craig was incredibly steady and supportive during this process, assuring me that I'd get through it and that I was safe and loved. But I felt out of my depth and so very alone. I wondered whether anyone else had been through it. And if they had, why didn't they talk about it? Where was the map I needed to navigate my way through this?

I did all I could to release this previously dormant grief and rage. It wasn't pretty, but I navigated the process in the best way I knew, although at times I wasn't able to bring my best self forward. It was on these occasions that I thought again of the mystics of old and longed to be able to retreat to that cave in the wilderness. But you can't hang out in a cave for months on end when your baby is waking you up 10 times a night and you're trying to run a business in the changing climate of a global pandemic!

## HEALING OUR ANCESTRAL LINES

Desperate for some professional help in navigating what would become the most difficult period of my life, I prayed deeply for the right support to come, and in time, it did. Somatic therapy helped me to regulate my nervous system and get out of fight, flight, freeze mode, which stopped my autoimmune flare-ups, and my health significantly improved from here. I also benefited from learning about the link between chronic autoimmune illnesses, nervous system dysregulation, and the repressed emotions that we've not felt safe enough to express.

And so, the silver lining of this challenging time was that the more the rage erupted in me, the more my body seemed to come back to life. Within the year, my longstanding chronic fatigue and insulin resistance both went into remission.

I was referred to Bob Jacobs, a naturopath with decades of experience in functional medicine, who ran some tests and changed my diet after discovering I was a celiac and allergic to foods I was regularly eating. This shift seemed to ease my body as it was no longer under attack and in an inflammatory state.

I'll never forget the day I told him about the surges of energy and rage and the spontaneous shaking I was experiencing at night. He looked at me, paused, and then asked if I'd heard of a Kundalini Shakti awakening. My breath taken, I smiled, and we shared an extended moment of silent recognition as two souls in the depths of the spiritual journey. I started crying at the Grace that had brought us together.

Bob told me that he could support my body by making the releasing a little less intense physically, but that ultimately, each journey is unique and that if I was on it, my soul knew how to get through it. He encouraged me to connect with Grace when I felt the surges of energy move through my system and suggested I repeat the sacred Sanskrit mantra 'om nama shivaya,' which I knew well from my kirtan training and was relieved to be reminded of. I whispered *om nama shivaya* day and night on those colonized lands on which I would eventually be born.

I found a gifted trauma specialist called Kay Dayton, who did a combination of therapies, including Tension and Trauma Release (TRE) and brainspotting (BSP). Over the months we worked together we noticed that it was as if my body was processing intergenerational trauma – the transmission of trauma between generations of a family – particularly crimes against the feminine and the severing of the Earth-based wisdom teachings of my ancestry.

As my body moved, I saw scenes and discovered stories about my Scottish ancestors being forced off their land when it was sold from beneath them for farming sheep. I saw women from my Irish ancestry being deported on ships to faraway countries to be wives, and others so hungry and desperate that their only option was to steal food to feed their families. I saw the utterly tragic devastation that occurred on those colonized lands too. Navigating the complexities of identity and history can be challenging, but by acknowledging and engaging with these truths, I saw hope for a more honest and inclusive dialogue about the legacies of colonialism, oppression, and inequality. My sensitivity was heightened to confront these difficult truths toward fostering healing.

I saw women and men being drowned and burned during the witch hunts of the Middle Ages. I saw countless women being shamed and sent away; their babies taken from them. Kay held a pristine space for this processing to happen and as she did, my nights became less intense, and I was able to get more sleep.

Kay told me that while conducting research into her own ancestry, she'd discovered that not only did she and I share the Campbell ancestral line, but she also shared the ancestral line of my husband and children. I was left in awe of the incredible odds and circumstances that had brought us together to heal our ancestral lines. I'm forever grateful for the support she gave me during this period.

At the same time, two of my long-term students, Coral **Scarlett** and Carrie Smith, shared with me an incredible story. They had met many years earlier in my online membership, The Sanctuary. Living far apart in different cities, they'd nevertheless developed a deep friendship and made regular trips to spend time together and support each other in Divine Feminine and ancestral healing. One day they discovered that they were in fact cousins, and for all those years, had been doing this mother line healing work together!

I also learned from the writing of Layne Redmond that because all the eggs a woman will ever carry in her ovaries are formed while she's a four-month-old fetus in her mother's womb, our cellular life (as an egg) actually begins in the womb of our grandmother. Each one of us spent five months in our grandmother's womb and she in turn formed in the womb of *her* grandmother. And she, her grandmother. On and on the chain goes, all the way back down the mother line to the Original Mother.

I also noticed the connection between the science of intergenerational trauma and what many Indigenous and mystical teachings speak of regarding healing the mother line and intergenerational healing seven generations forward and back. I also saw that this echoed with my own mystical experience with the Ancient Grandmothers of the Earth and the Great Mother years earlier. I'll talk more about healing the mother line in Part II.

## SOUL INQUIRY

*What is the ancient feminine within you calling you to do?*

Lay all of your fears on my altar.
Let the winds of change
blow as they may.
Let them toss your hair,
slap your face.
Let them leave you disheveled,
disorientated, and unsure where to turn.

I will be here, waiting in
the deep cave of your heart.
By the light which,
no matter what happens,
still shines bright.
Take shelter here.

*the great mother* △

△

# THAT'S A BRAVE SOUL

The most compassionate people are those who have descended to the underworld and returned with the pearl. For it takes being broken to be truly open. The ones who are avoiding the pain, their hearts are the most closed off. They struggle to be around those who suffer for extended periods, for like brings up like and the depths remind them of what they're not yet able to face. The least compassionate people are those who do everything possible to avoid their pain.

What if we were taught in school that if we track back far enough, we'll find we all came from the same mother? And that when we see someone struggling, instead of regarding them as weak and urging them to be strong, we should say: 'That's a brave soul before me.' We're all from the same human line. What if, instead of inviting someone to pull themselves together as quickly as possible and be strong, we thank them for doing this work, saying: 'I see what you're doing. I thank you. I honor you.' For they're doing it on behalf of humanity and that means they're doing it on behalf of you, too.

There are ancient places and times where those who had journeyed through a dark night were supported and fed, encouraged, comforted, and revered. They were recognized for the great courageous journey that their soul had chosen to embark on. Not all souls do this. But more and more are. Is one of them you? They're the visionaries, the artists, the healers, the wise ones. With the right conditions they'll return with the pearl from which we'll all benefit.

## SOUL INQUIRY

*Who in your life deserves to be acknowledged*
*for their courage? (And it can be you.)*

Sometimes when we're hollowed out,
it's so that in times to come,
others can find refuge there.
Let the hollowing happen.
It's how you find your wholeness.

*making of the healer* ◬

△

# YOUR GRIEF SHOWS YOU
# HOW MUCH YOU LOVE

Your grief is evidence of how much you love. So, when grief comes, give it as many breaths as it needs. Give it as many days as it needs. Give it as many years as it needs. The agony your grief shows is the thread of the connection between you and the one who once was. What if your grief is love that's looking where to go?

The incarnation process isn't easy. When we experience loss of any kind, part of us always aches for the person, thing, or identity that's no longer here. But no matter how hard we try to cling to that which was, it's just not possible. Ask anyone who has loved and lost and then tried to live as they did before.

The first time I properly experienced grief was when my friend Blair passed away suddenly at the age of 29. For a period of more than a year my heart physically ached. I'll never forget the feeling I had one spring morning when I left my London apartment and realized that everything was continuing just the way it had the day before. The sun was still shining, bins were being emptied, joggers were jogging, buses and trains were running. My world had been ripped apart, and I was offended that the rest of the world hadn't altered to reflect that.

For someone quite young, I'd experienced the deaths of an unusually high number of friends, and so grief and loss was not foreign to me, but there was something about Blair's soul leaving that broke my heart wide open. I recall a feeling in that first year of both hating and loving the grief simultaneously. I longed for a time when it wouldn't hurt so bad, and yet there was also a sense of deep love and intimacy and connection in this grief. Looking back now I can see it's because the two are related – the love and the sorrow. The depth of my love for Blair was echoed in the depth of my grief.

Not long after Blair's death, Wildcat, another good friend from our tight-knit friendship group, died unexpectedly and then my relationship of more than 10 years ended. This cracked my heart open even further, and I think the loss of the relationship made me question it all and feel more alone on this journey.

And, in this aloneness, in one of the darkest winters I'd ever been through, when it felt like all the lights had gone out, I couldn't shake the subtle sense that it was actually *in* this darkness, at the rock bottom of my life, in the ascent of my awakening, that I could feel my connection with spirit and my inner light stronger than ever before. It was as if my grief had caused the strength of my personal will to step aside and my soul to step more fully in.

Soon after this period of grieving, I gathered up the courage to leave my job and follow my soul's calling as a mystical writer. And although it took a lot of hard work, it felt like the Spirit of Life was from that time onward on my side. Maybe you've felt it too – in those moments on the bathroom floor or while sitting alone in your car, when grief cracks your heart wide open, and things get really still. As much as it hurts, you're most certainly living.

> *Through our grief we grow. It's in this moment that we're brought face-to-face with the agony of separation, and at the same time we awaken to an intimate connection with all things in life.*

In our denial of death and loss, of aging and decay, we've forgotten the great death mysteries. And death mysteries are birth mysteries. Rebirth mysteries. Life mysteries. Law of the Earth mysteries. Without them, life doesn't survive. With them, it thrives. It's possible to be born anew over and over again, and our grief can show us how. It's in the initiation of grief that a portal opens and our hearts have the opportunity to be stretched open wide enough for our souls to take up residency. And when this happens it invites more life in. We're invited to become more alive in the process of grief.

Sometimes, when our life crumbles, so do the walls of separation within our own hearts. Our wailing reverberates to the ends of the Universe, calling lost parts of our souls back home. And the four chambers of our hearts unite with the One. Sometimes, while we're in this excruciating, liberating state, dormant parts of our soul awaken from their slumber and come online. They return to us, and we more fully plant ourselves here.

And as our minds cannot fathom what's happened, the portal opens once more, and it's given a unique opportunity to surrender ever so slightly, allowing the mystery of Life to whisper to it and through it. Lives and worlds can change in an instant. We can awaken in an instant.

Our grief can return us to the spiral, the natural flow of Life. At the initiatory gateway of grief, the mind is blown, and the heart's intelligence is invited home. It's in the initiation of grief that our willpower weakens and our defenses drop, allowing a pathway for the soul to occupy the cells more than before.

Of course, the opposite can also happen. If we truly are alone in our grief, our souls can choose little by little not to be present for it. This is called soul loss. Which is why we must sit alongside the grieving for as long as it takes. Not to see the grieving as something to fix but as someone to encourage, hold, and love. Celebrating how much they love. Reminding them that this is an initiation to invite the soul in more fully. And if they do, soon, soon, soon, in a way deeper than before, they will truly live.

## SOUL INQUIRY

*Think about the times in your life when you've experienced grief. What has your grief taught you about life? If you're grieving right now, what does your grief want you to know?*

*Morning* is on the other side of *mourning*.
*Healing* is on the other side of *feeling*.
*Rebirth* is on the other side of *death*.

Everything in this world begins again.
If you have the courage to let it properly end.

*beginning again* △

Δ

# LAY IT ON THE ALTAR

To keep ourselves steady when times are turbulent, we need something to hold on to. When things are crumbling around us, we must find something we can count on that won't budge. Deep roots for when the winds of change come a-blowing. A supportive community for when we don't believe we can make it on our own.

When we leave home, we must find something new to hold us. When our lover leaves, when the job ends, when our parents die, we must find something new to hold us. When we think that there's nothing holding us, it's an invitation to find new, supportive ground, and in most cases that ground is found within ourselves and the gravity of the ground that's forever been holding us. The one companion who can never be taken from you has always been you.

*This is always the invitation of loss and separation. To discover the sureness of the soil. The holding of the roots.*

Sometimes, life rips from us what we cling to the most; perhaps we cling to it because we can feel the cycles of change coming. Yet in our longest, darkest nights, we discover that it's in the empty spaces that we can be reached and held the most. It's in these that we find a holding that we didn't know before. We see that gravity has always been holding us and that instead of looking around for another to save us, we can take the child within into the rose of our own hearts or fall into our own laps.

We can be so tough on ourselves, but it's through our challenges, mistakes, and life changes that we grow the most. And when we experience these difficult times, we gain the capacity to truly be there for another when the going gets tough for them. Think back on your life and you'll find the truth waiting for you there. The deepest connection is always on the other side of the deepest separation.

No one is immune to the challenges of life, and we all need support as we journey through it. To find proper ground along the bumpiest of roads. To know what can truly hold us. To find a way to soften toward ourselves when life's hard and the winter brutally cold. To lay all that we're carrying on the altar of life and trust that we're held.

## GREAT MOTHER ACTIVATION

*I release all that I'm carrying, especially that which was never mine to carry, on the altar, and I set myself free.*

△
# RECEIVING SUPPORT

In the past, receiving support wasn't something that came naturally to me – to be honest, it made me feel out of control and uncomfortable. As someone who had been overly independent from a young age, I found asking for and receiving support extremely difficult, which is why in the descent phase of my awakening journey, any spiritual practice that involved opening up to receiving and surrendering was so powerful.

While I was deeply grieving the sudden deaths of two friends and the end of my long-term relationship, and it felt like my whole life was falling apart, several friends kept offering support, saying things like 'Is there anything I can do? Can I come and make you a cup of tea?' However, although I would have loved to have my friends' company, I struggled to accept their offers of support, thinking, *I'm capable of making myself a cup of tea!* But then, through both of my births and postpartum periods I kept being invited to deepen my ability to call in and receive support.

One month after her birth, my daughter Goldie was diagnosed with hip dysplasia, and we had to travel to a hospital two hours from our home twice or three times a week for treatment and scans. My postpartum support had ended, and my mum had returned to Australia, and we were flung out of our gentle newborn bubble.

Goldie had to wear a brace 24/7, which made basic tasks like changing her nappy and breastfeeding that much harder. A sweet-natured baby, she took it in her stride and complained only when it was very uncomfortable. The only time we could remove the brace was to bathe her and that was limited to 30 minutes a day. The kind nurses showed me how to ensure it was fitted correctly, keeping her legs in an 'M' position – kind of like a squatting frog or a woman in labor – in the hope that her hip sockets would deepen, and her legs wouldn't remain dislocated.

I was exhausted from the round-the-clock feeding, the long drives to the hospital, and a violent cough caused by long COVID. One Friday after we'd had dinner at a pub in town, Sunny had a meltdown and so I picked him up and carried him all the way home while Craig pushed Goldie in the stroller. Later, while lifting Sunny into the bath, I felt a sudden drop in my pelvic floor, and I started to panic.

On seeing a doctor, I found out that my pelvic floor had prolapsed quite severely. I dove into support groups, podcasts, and books and discovered that more than 30 percent of women will experience some degree of pelvic prolapse in their lifetimes and yet little is offered in the form of prevention, education, treatment, or support. I felt that ancient Sacred Feminine rage bubbling up again and wondered if this was a condition that affected men, would the situation be the same.

I couldn't understand how something that commonly develops in the aftermath of pregnancy and childbirth could be so shockingly unsupported and not widely spoken about. Why didn't anyone tell me this could happen? How did I not know about the risks of lifting my toddler in the postpartum period while having a chronic cough?

I was unable to lift Goldie or take her car seat out of the car, so after a few weeks, my mum flew back from Australia to stay with us and help me with the weekly hospital visits. But the real medicine was my mum's presence in general. She made me cups of tea while I was feeding Goldie and looked after her between 8 and 9 a.m. each morning so I could do the pelvic floor exercises my physio had given me. While she was around, I began to thrive. And because I was thriving, Goldie was too. It was the healing nectar I so needed after not having my mum around when Sunny was born because of the pandemic.

One cluster-feeding night, Goldie woke for probably her tenth feed, and Mum came into my room and sat on the chair to keep me company. When Goldie had finished and was fast asleep, Mum went to leave, but then she sat back down, saying, 'I'll just wait until you're both asleep.' And she did; she just sat there, watching over me watching over my daughter, her granddaughter.

It's a moment and a feeling that's etched so deeply into every one of my cells. I saw the rings of holding which we all need but so rarely receive. A web of support, love, and holding that I believe we're all ravenous for, but which is so often absent in our modern world. Looking back now I see that what my mum was doing was essentially mothering me, and because I was being mothered it was that much easier to mother my daughter. The layers of support could be felt on a cellular level.

We've built a world that's devoid of community and disconnected from the Earth that holds us. With a bit of perspective, I realize now that it took my body and my daughter's body to cry out in urgency for me to allow myself to receive the mothering and support that I didn't know I so deeply needed. I wonder, if all our mothers and all the mothers of the world had received deep layers of support in those early years, would we be less disconnected and separate? If we saw women as Goddess and the Earth as our Mother and nature as an extension of that, what type of world would this be?

## SOUL INQUIRY

*What support do you most want to call into your life?*

*If you knew you would be supported, what would you do?*

# △
# AFTER THE RAIN

There's something very special and sacred about the moment after it stops raining. The atmosphere has released all that it was holding, and in turn, the Earth has been cleansed, replenished, and nourished. It's a feeling like the one we have in the moment after we stop crying. As those salty, healing waters fall, they activate oxytocin and endorphins, which create a shift in how we feel. What was once overwhelming now seems possible. And while we may not know it consciously, noticeable growth will soon follow.

Emotions are soothed. Broken hearts are on the mend. Times of trial are coming to an end. Mercy can be felt. There's a moment of relief. There's hope on the horizon. A new, encouraging silver lining can now be made out. What's been challenging and difficult has or is about to ease up.

If you've been going through a challenging time, know that soon, soon, soon things will ease. It's the Law of the Earth. These past weeks, months, or even years haven't been straightforward. They've likely asked you to dig deep and endure hardships that have tested you, but there are always smoother seas ahead. The confusing currents always shift. What you've learned and how you've grown can never be taken from your soul. When they come, enjoy the warmth of the blessings that Life has for you. Glorious new beginnings aren't just possible but certain, after the rain.

## SOUL INQUIRY

*What have you been through that deserves to be celebrated?*

through *mourning,*
*morning* will come.

△

# MORNING HAS COME

For several years my nights were devoid of mystical dreams, but then they returned with a recurring one in which I saw myself in a desert-like cave deep in the belly of the Earth. Above me were thousands of bees and around me were ancient temple medicine women whose symbol was the bee. Soon after, I learned of an ancient lineage known as the bee priestesses, which I believe may have been the women I saw in this dream.

I was shown that the descent phase of my awakening journey, the dark nights of the soul, was finally coming to an end and that the bee was my symbol for that period of transformation. The yellow of the bee represented the sweetness of Life – the honey, the ecstasy, the joy, the bud, the bloom, the bliss, the spring, the summer. The black represented the darkest of nights, the underworld, my feminine power, the ancient ancestral grief, the agony, the loss, the holding, the surrender, the fall, the winter.

The medicine women shared how nothing new can be born in the light, that the fertile void of the darkness is the powerful portal through which everything is reborn. And that transformation isn't possible without it. Rebirth isn't possible without it.

I saw my daughter and my son and was deeply moved by the unique energy that they each had come in with. Sunny arrived on Earth with incredible depth and potent purity. I saw how he was the one who had stretched my heart so much wider than before. I saw the depths of his soul and the soul agreement we made for him to come at such an intense time. I saw Goldie and the golden nectar that she came in with. The bringer of the honey for us all. Our teacher to find the sacred sweetness in the simplicity, the joy that's available to us every moment of every day.

I saw how huge an activator and healer Sunny was and how Goldie's entrance into this world with me as her mother had not been possible without Sunny coming first and clearing the way. I was shown the gates of Life once more and how this journey to which the soul says yes isn't a small thing. The bees then hummed the vibration of the heart, causing all the residual pain, grief, and trauma to be released from within my cells, flesh, and organs as black liquid left my body and was transmuted and cleared.

I woke up feeling relieved, humbled, and in awe of the huge journey I'd been on. The next morning, as I drove down a country lane on the way home from a somatic therapy session, listening to 'Take Me to Church' by Sinéad O'Connor, who had just passed, I had that familiar feeling that something was about to happen.

As Sinéad sang, I felt a final powerful surge of energy begin to move through me and travel down my mother line. Overcome by the most ferocious, sweet, tender, and holy feminine power I sang the song down my mother line. In honor of them and all that they had endured. I sang for them. I sang for my daughter, and I sang for me.

As I did, I felt the power of my soul, life-force, and the Spirit of Life fully occupy my body, from the top of my head right down to my toes. I could feel myself returning from the underworld completely transformed. No part of me was left unchanged. I felt the Ancient Grandmothers of the Earth and the Great Mother too and how this whole time they had never left my side. I saw the sacred that was always here all around me, below me, above me, and within me.

The darkest night was over, and the light of a new morning had finally come.

Toes hanging over the edge
she realized:

The end is also the beginning.
And the beginning cannot fully begin
without the end fully ending.

Deep breath.
Let go.
Leap.

*second bloom* △

Part Two

# YOU'RE GOING
## *somewhere*
# SACRED

*Understanding That Change Is Part of Life
and Healing Is Always Happening*

The grief cracked her heart wide open,
creating room for her soul to breathe.
The space caused the treasure within her chest
to open and her soul's dream to be seen.

*the medicine of grief* △

△

# HEALING IS ALWAYS HAPPENING

Healing is always happening. Nature is always changing. We are part of nature, and so we are always changing too. We are ever-changing beings in an ever-changing world. And because we're always changing, we're always in a state of healing. Returning again and again to wholeness, every moment of every day.

Wholeness isn't a static state, because we are part of nature and nature is always changing, growing, and transforming. What if we saw wholeness not as a fixed, perfect state but as an at-oneness with Life itself? With nature itself. And because nature doesn't stay in one perfect, static state, we'd remember that we're not designed to do that either.

I wonder, is it our obsession with being forever in full bloom that makes us feel broken when things change for us... when we experience anything other than what's seen as ideal? What I want you to know is that you're not broken, and you never were; you're simply part of the ever-changing nature of Life. Change is your natural state.

*You were never meant to be one single shape, size, or way. You're always becoming more and more of who you truly are.*

Healing is always happening. Every moment of every day. Your body knows how to heal. Your mind knows how to heal. Your heart knows how to heal. Your soul knows how to heal. Your cells know how to heal. Life is always changing. You are part of Life, and so you are always changing too. Healing is happening. Change is your natural state.

No one is immune to the polarity of this human experience. The only way through it is to embrace all its parts – from the ecstasy to the agony, the joy to the grief, the bloom to the fall. Let it stretch you wide open. When you do this, you'll realize that healing is always happening, and Life is on your side. Right now, and in every single moment, healing IS happening.

## SOUL INQUIRY

*If you didn't see yourself as unhealed or*
*broken, what would you do?*

# half one thing, half the next.

I don't know who I am anymore.
I'm half one thing, half the next.
The only place I can find ground is within.
But even that part of me feels like it's in flux.

I know I'm part of the cosmos and that
the cosmos is self-organizing.
But it's also beautiful chaos and I feel
more chaos than order right now.

Maybe the chaos is the chrysalis.
The great mystery reorganizing itself.
The more you try to make sense of it,
the more random it feels.

The moment I find something that defines
who I'm becoming, it slips through my fingers.
The only thing left to do is to
stop clinging and to let it all fall.
To lay who I once was and will soon be on the
altar of the great mystery, wait, and simply be.
As my soul readies itself to express yet another
part of my multidimensionality.

# △
# THE MYSTERIOUS TIMING
# OF HEALING

Through feeling, healing will always come. Healing is often a slow, steady process. It's complex, not linear. It takes as long as it takes. And most of the time, that's much longer than we would wish. However, like all things in nature, there's a mysterious intelligence to healing. And if we trust it and let the once-vibrant petals fall to the Earth, cut back what's no longer, and protect the buds from being pried open, we may find ourselves in a second bloom. And fruit will follow. We can't manufacture that. We must trust the great mystery in the process.

The buds somehow manage to burst through by opening to Life. Contraction then expansion. When we're going through a time of healing – growth, transformation, change, rebirth – the challenge is not to close ourselves off from the world but somehow courageously open through the difficulty, the fear, the unknown, the hurt. And when we feel safe enough, to let Life soften not harden us, let it deepen and cradle us. To reach for what's holding us through the change. To deepen our relationship with that which can never be extinguished or leave us – the great light of the soul. To trust that Life will always usher us through.

## SOUL INQUIRY

*If you trusted Life a little bit more, what would you do?*

The winds of change are coming.

The winds of change are near.

The winds of change are coming.

The winds of change are here.

*nature* △

# △
# EVER CHANGING

Change is the only constant in life. The one sure, certain thing. The intelligent pulse of Life isn't static. It's always changing. Now, now, now. We're only ever meant to change.

Nature shows us how to embrace change every moment of every day. Change is difficult for the mind, which often strives for one perfect state, tends to fixate on the past or the future, and tries to control life and bend things to our will. Everything changes. Even the most ancient, barren, dry desert cave was once a cathedral for the fish of the deep ocean floor.

We're cyclic beings in a constant state of change, of evolution, of transformation, of growth. When you resist your ever-changing, cyclic nature, you resist Life and eventually find yourself feeling stuck. Emotionally, mentally, physically, and energetically. When you resist change, you cut yourself off from life-force itself. This is why we feel stuck, for we're stagnant and resisting Life's natural flow.

We're living in a time when we've been raised to see ourselves as separate from nature and the Earth. But we are part of nature, part of the Earth. And it's our disconnection from the Earth and her seasons that leads us to believe that we should be in full bloom all year round, and that we should grow, grow, grow without leaving space to cut back. When we focus on the never-ending bloom, we forget the importance of all of life's phases. We resist and miss the great initiation that autumn (fall) and winter bring. But nature is teaching us this every day. She's forever showing us how to embrace the everchanging seasons of our life.

We're not meant to stay the same. Relationships aren't meant to stay the same. Life isn't meant to stay the same. Nothing on this planet is meant to stay the same. The seasons teach us that. Night and day teach us that. Time and age teach us that. Birth and death teach us that. We may return to a place, a person, but things won't ever be exactly as they were, for everything and everyone is ever changing.

*Nothing is static in this corner of the cosmos.*
*The more we try to control things and keep*
*them the same, the further away we become*
*from the flow of Life and ourselves.*

Change can be scary, for it means surrendering to the unknown of continually gathering the courage to exist in the in-between. To being not who you were yet not quite who you'll soon become. It requires a trust in the transformation and we're always transforming. A trust in the death, for the rebirth to occur.

The more we resist change, the further away we get from who we're becoming. The more we resist change, the more disconnected from life-force and Life we become. When we embrace change, we embrace Life and nature and are forever becoming. It's what the soul came here for. It's the bridge between spirit and matter. It came here to truly live.

So much of the suffering in our lives stems from our relationship with change. We tend to switch from one state to the next – either WANTING things to change or NOT WANTING things to change; wanting things to be different or wanting them to remain the same. But the harsh truth of life, and the wisdom on offer if we can surrender to it, is that there's no constant. There's only change. So, how do we befriend it? This is a lifetime's work.

Before each of my births, I felt such a sense of change as I entered the days that I call the in-between. When we're no longer who we were but we're also not yet who we soon will be. I'd experienced this in my life metaphorically at key periods of my awakening journey, but childbirth made it palpably clear. I learned that for initiation (change) to happen, in order for us to truly transform, we must fully surrender who we once were in order to be born anew. And that for something new to begin, something old must fall away.

## SOUL INQUIRY

*How are you being called to embrace change right now?*

# roll away the stone

She was half one thing, half the next.
Transforming.
Morphing by the minute.

Surrendering the petals to the Earth for the
chance of a second bloom.
She was in the exquisite, messy
gunk of her becoming.

An equal mix of hope and grief.
Excitement and terror.
Resistance and acceptance.
Mourning and dawn.

She was dying while still fully living.
It was right in the middle of her life that
she gave birth to herself.
Hallelujah!
Roll away the stone!

# △
# INNER AND OUTER SEASONS

*'Look deep into nature, and then you'll understand everything better.'*

ALBERT EINSTEIN

Nature is a mystery school for the soul and the seasons are our greatest teacher. They hold within them the codes to cyclic living, and they show us how to embrace change and transformation. Over and over again, they show us how to be reborn, how to die while still fully living. When we embrace the changing seasons, we say yes to transformation and rebirth. If we see ourselves as an interconnected part of nature, then as the seasons change, we know that it's possible for us to change too.

The most transformative work I've ever done, and it didn't occur until my third decade, was developing a relationship with the seasons. Prior to that I was often out of sync with the pulse of Life and my feminine power. Decades spent attempting to be in full bloom all year round, just as society had taught me to, and making it in a man's world had led to burnout, chronic illness, and a way of living that didn't fit my soul. However, right in front of my eyes were the secrets of the authentic life that my soul so craved.

During my first Kundalini Shakti awakening in 2012, I began to see the codes and the Spirit of Life within nature. I couldn't believe I hadn't noticed them before. Everything became so much more alive, and I could see how interconnected everything is. I'd walk in nature and write while communing with the plants, trees, and flowers. This daily practice was the foundation where I really started to receive the medicine of the seasons and began connecting with the consciousness of plants.

As the trees gathered the courage to loosen their grip on their leaves in the fall, I was inspired to loosen my grip on my need to bend life to my individualistic will. In spring, as the daffodils courageously burst through the frosty soil, hope and determination were stoked within me. In summer, as the roses softened and released the very thing that attracted others to them for the chance of a second bloom, I was reminded of the necessity to create space for something new to be born. And as the honeysuckle called in the bee with its scent, I was reminded to slow down and savor the sweetness.

I also studied the traditions of my ancestry, including the Celtic Wheel of the Year; however, it wasn't until I moved to Glastonbury in 2018 that honoring the seasons became an inherent part of my everyday life. I started gathering with others to celebrate these seasonal shifts and introduced ritual and ceremony into my days. I hadn't realized how hungry for it I was.

This simple change wasn't a spiritual practice that I needed to do; it was a rhythmic way of living that enabled me to enter a sacred relationship with the Spirit of Life. The more deeply I followed the Wheel of the Year, the more connected I became to the wisdom of my ancestry and the more I felt held, supported, and as if I truly belonged.

## THE MEDICINE OF THE INNER AND OUTER SEASONS

I noticed that as cyclic beings who are part of the land around us and move through the seasons of spring, summer, fall, winter each year, we also experience *inner* seasons – the phases that we cycle through internally throughout our lives. I reflected on how my dark nights of the soul phase felt like the depths of winter. When everything's cut back, barren, and seemingly frozen, it seems as if nothing will ever grow again. However, deep beneath the hard soil, there's activity. And if we allow ourselves to be cloaked by the darkness of the long winter nights, we'll discover that soon, soon, soon, the buds of spring will return. And after that, so will the flower and the fruit.

I recalled going through another 'inner winter' between 2010 and 2012, when my life crumbled. It was in the darkness of that time that I finally answered the deepest call of my soul and started sharing my writing in a way that was much more public than before. I went on to quit my corporate career to focus on my writing full-time and six months after that, I received my first publishing contract.

It was through embracing both the inner and outer winter of this period of my life that I was able to fully enter my inner spring and then summer. During my last month in my job, I met Craig, and a year later we got engaged. My first book was published as I entered my inner summer. After getting married in Australia, I returned to the UK and began deepening my work into the feminine mysteries. This was my inner autumn, and the fires of my feminine power began to be stoked.

The more deeply we understand the characteristics of the outer seasons and the changes they require of nature (remembering that we are nature and that the seasons are inviting these changes within us too), the more easily we can navigate the inner season we're currently in and what it's asking of us.

*If you develop a relationship with*
*the seasons, you'll never be without*
*anything to guide you, for you'll find a*
*wise teacher waiting for you there.*

As we move through the inner seasons of our lives, it may not look as if much is happening, but inside us, deep transformation is taking place. In both my personal life and my work, I've come to understand how helpful it is to know and acknowledge which inner season we're in because just like the outer seasons, each inner season bears its own gifts and challenges.

The inner seasons of spring and summer have a more 'masculine' energy that allows us to manifest, to go out into the world and achieve. It's the energy that we see in the natural world in the outer seasons of spring and summer, with life-force shooting up from the ground and sap rising in the trees. When we're in an inner spring or summer, this is the energy that's moving through us – new life, new ideas, the ability to initiate things, asserting our will, and showing up in the world in full force.

The energy of inner spring and summer can be wonderfully productive, and we can find great fulfillment in sharing our gifts. However, those of us who have been raised in a toxic capitalist world in which there's so much focus on this kind of energy, often forget the importance of the other inner seasons we move through.

The inner seasons of autumn and winter bring a more interior energy, which is also much more feminine. Just as we retreat into the warmth and safety of our homes during the outer seasons of autumn and winter, so these inner seasons invite us to retreat further into ourselves. To take a journey into our own consciousness and be more private as we navigate our ever-changing inner landscape.

If you're aware that you're in an inner winter, you'll know not to push – patience, tenderness, and stillness are required more than anything else. You move from trying to assert 'my will' to being open to and accepting of 'thy will,' allowing things to unfold in their own way, with their own divine timing. On the following pages is an overview of the qualities of both the inner and outer seasons.

## THE MEDICINE OF SPRING

**Feminine archetype**: Maiden.

**The medicine**: new beginnings, planting seeds, getting ready to bloom, tending your dreams, upward energy, excitement, hope, potential, inspiration.

**Feels**: exciting, full of promise.

**Journaling prompts**: What lights you up? What's your soul calling you to do? What's your heart's deepest prayer? If you knew you'd be supported, what would you do? What's your secret dream? What do you want to experience next? How can you truly live?

## THE MEDICINE OF SUMMER

**Feminine archetype**: Mother or Goddess.

**The medicine**: blooming, opening to life, saying yes, pleasure, joy, tasting the sweetness of life, rapture, ecstasy, adventure, energy, solar, warmth, enjoyment, social, play, fun, creativity.

**Feels**: full of life, energy, and adventure.

**Journaling prompts**: What's rising in you? What are you being called to create? If you were feeling abundant, what would you do? How can you say yes to life? What do you long to do just for fun? What's blooming within you? What brings you pleasure? What are you being called to embrace?

## THE MEDICINE OF AUTUMN (FALL)

**Feminine archetype**: Wild Woman or Dark Feminine.

**The medicine**: letting go, wildness, realignment, courage, falling away, loosening your grip, harnessing your inner power, frustration, sacred rage, alchemy, taking your place, reaping what you've sown.

**Feels**: powerful and perhaps daunting.

**Journaling prompts**: What's falling away? What are you clinging on to for fear of nothing coming to take its place? If you weren't afraid of your power, what would you do? How are you being called to transmute your sacred rage into something productive?

## THE MEDICINE OF WINTER

**Feminine archetype**: Grandmother or Elder.

**The medicine**: initiation, rebirth, renewal, rest, going underground, the fertile void, surrender, mystery, unknowing, death, the end is also the beginning, union.

**Feels**: like nothing will ever grow again; a yearning for rest and quiet.

**Journaling prompts**: How are you being called to slow down? What new seeds are you being called to nurture? How are you being called to rest? What does the wise part of you want you to know?

## SOUL INQUIRY

*Which outer season are you in right now?*
*What is this season encouraging you to embrace?*

*Which inner season do you feel you're in right now?*
*How are you being called to embrace this a little more?*

She prepared for her death
each and every f a l l.
For she knew that
if she did,
come spring,
again and again,
she would be
reborn.

*the mystery school of nature* △

# △
# HONORING ENDINGS AND THE
# FERTILE VOID OF NEW BEGINNINGS

It's impossible to live a life and not experience endings. It's impossible to live a life and not experience loss. It's impossible to live a life and not experience change. Yet, most of us are never taught the importance of endings. How to honor them and navigate them.

In a world that's so focused on the new and operating at a fast pace, we've forgotten the importance of honoring endings, and we don't take the time to acknowledge these moments of completion. Sometimes this is because it's painful to accept that an ending is taking place, or because we're racing to the next thing, attempting to be in bloom all year round.

We find endings difficult. We ask ourselves who we'll be without this person or thing in our lives. What will come to take their place? But we're ever-changing beings and we're not meant to stay the same. The choice is yours – you can loosen your grip and let the waves carry you into shore or you can thrash against them. Either way, the tides of change will deliver you to the same place.

Before we begin anything, we must first end what's been – for us all to be fully there in the beginning of the new beginning. If we don't do this, part of us will become energetically stuck in the past and we'll find ourselves separated from the Spirit of Life. Endings are a time of change and transformation, and if we acknowledge and honor them properly, an initiation is possible. A transformation is possible. A rebirth is possible. But often, courage is required for the rebirth to happen.

We can look to nature for inspiration on how to allow this rebirth into our lives. Nature knows the importance of endings. Unless the rose finds the courage to release its petals to the wind, a second bloom cannot come, and neither can the fruit. The rose knows that we need to surrender what was to the Earth to one day be transformed.

Endings hurl us into the in-between. We're invited to go from something familiar to something unknown. Endings call us to the edge of our lives, where we discover that we cannot go back to the way things were, but it's not yet clear how things will be. All we can do is wait. And if we wait, if we gather up the courage to let them properly end, the dream of a new beginning will eventually call us forth.

I call this time the fertile void. It's inner winter medicine. In the fertile void of our lives, we're called to have patience and enter a state of deep rest, repair, regeneration, and acceptance. To let a part of our lives, or even who we once were, metaphorically die in order to seed, sprout, bud, and bloom again.

There's often a letting-go involved, and grief or mourning. A death of self or what once was. The ending of things that were once important: relationships, jobs, identities, ways of being. The fertile void asks that we honor endings so we can begin again. This is a crucial part of growth, and new growth isn't possible without it. Nature shows us again and again just how important this phase is. When we plant a seed in the dark, fertile womb of the soil, it's easy to mistake this stage of growth as one where nothing much is happening. But beneath the surface, things have never been more active.

*Trust the sureness of the soil. Be cradled by the great mystery. This is a very powerful time, and the new is already being woven without you having to micromanage every move.*

Western culture tends to bypass endings. We can see this when our well-meaning loved ones avoid witnessing an ending and rush to look for the silver lining instead. In some cases, this can be helpful; however, it can also lead us to feel unacknowledged, unwitnessed, and alone. And it's this feeling of aloneness, of disconnection, that can sometimes cause parts of us to become stuck in these unacknowledged moments in time.

This is especially true when we experience endings that aren't embedded within our society. For example, when someone dies, a funeral or wake are culturally recognized rituals that honor both the life of the deceased person and the end of the physical relationship the attendees had with them. However, when a friendship ends, we don't have rituals like this to help us move through the grief that may come with it. Without the witnessing or understanding, we're more likely to feel abandoned or alone. And the more alone we feel, the more difficult the ending can be.

Sometimes, endings can be traumatizing. Trauma happens when a person isn't emotionally witnessed during a distressing experience. Often, this can result in a part of them becoming lodged in the time and place of the traumatic event.

## CYCLIC ENDINGS

There are two main types of ending: cyclic and non-cyclic. Cyclic endings are cycle-based endings; examples include the end of a day, the end of a season, the end of a year. On your birthday you experience a cyclic ending of the 12 months since your last birthday. And when a person reaches menopause and their periods stop, that's a cyclic ending as well as the beginning of a new phase in their life. Here are some other examples of cyclic endings, many of which also mark a beginning.

- Becoming a parent
- Birth (your own birth, taking your first breath)

- Death (your own death, taking your last breath)
- Death of a loved one
- Leaving school, university, or training
- Menarche (first period)
- Menstruation
- The turning of the Wheel of the Year
- Your child starting or finishing nursery or school

## NON-CYCLIC ENDINGS

Non-cyclic endings are less predictable, so we may feel less prepared for them when they come. They can be divided into two further categories: endings that we instigate ourselves and endings that are beyond our control. Sometimes non-cyclic endings occur because someone has made a conscious choice to end something and sometimes the decision is unconscious. These endings may feel personal – for example, being let go from a job or a lover breaking up with you – or impersonal: a bolt of lightning damages your property, and you must leave the place where you live and start again somewhere else. Here are some more examples of non-cyclic endings:

- Ending of a friendship
- Divorce
- Break-up of a romantic relationship
- Child leaving home
- Completion of a creative project
- Moving abroad
- Termination of a job, career, or voluntary role
- Local friends or family relocating
- Loss of a particular identity

- You or a loved one becoming injured or ill or losing mental or physical capacity
- Moving home; the sale of a childhood home
- Receiving unexpected news (e.g. finding out that your partner has been unfaithful, discovering that you have a sibling you didn't know about, or becoming aware that something's different to what you believed)
- Stopping a particular pastime, e.g. retiring from a sport or passion

May we honor our endings for ourselves and for one another.

## SOUL INQUIRY

*Has there been an ending in your life*
*that wasn't honored properly?*

*What did the younger you need to hear or experience*
*in that moment to help you move on?*

*What do you need to do now to honor that ending properly?*

# i'm not who i thought i was

I've been a thousand different people.
And I long for the space and freedom to
be someone different than them.
Not who I once was or will someday be.

The me I'm becoming, not the one they think I am.
She's dead to me. I light candles for her and who
she was, for without her I would not be.
But she isn't me.

Let me be in the messy in-between.
In the gunk of my expansion.
Let me be beautiful not pretty, for pretty isn't real.
I long to be in the freedom of my becoming.
Not who people say I am,
but who I really am in real time.

I long for the space to be in the not knowing
without having to explain myself to anyone.
As I purge all that's been locked within me,
so much is coming up that isn't me.
And it needs to, if I'm to be free.

They say you have a whole new body every seven years.
I wonder, is it possible to know who you
are when you are actually in it?

Maybe the moment you try to define it,
you are no longer that person.
Maybe all that's left for me to do is
to embrace the mystery of me.
Cell of the cosmos.
Chaos and order existing at the same time.

# △
# THE ACHE OF GROWING APART

When the people we're in relationship with fail to grow alongside us, we can experience an unspeakable grief. Maybe one of you has changed and not the other or you both have, but in different directions and ways. The love is present and you're still there in the physical, but the more time that goes by, the further apart you feel.

Why doesn't anyone talk about the ache of growing apart? It's much easier to mourn and be witnessed in the kind of grief that's more clear-cut.

The ache of growing apart is hard to understand, but it's real. Accepting the change can take some time. But once expectations are released, the love can be freed. And as the petals of what was once so fragrant and alive fall to the soil, they become the very nourishment the seeds of tomorrow need to spring, bud, and bloom.

## SOUL INQUIRY

*Have you felt the ache of growing apart
from someone in your life?*

*Who do you feel far apart from right now?*

*Is there anything you're being called to do?*

△

# WHEN FRIENDSHIPS END

Relationships are how we grow. And they're how we make sense of the world. They help us navigate the ever-changing seasons of our lives and they *create* a lot of the changing seasons of our lives. They show us who we are and who we're not. They invite us to return to ourselves and find more meaning in our lives.

We don't talk often enough about the special type of grief that can arise when a friendship ends. When a friendship ends there's no funeral, no divorce papers, and there are rarely any condolences. We know that some friendships are meant to be for a lifetime and some for a season, and that as we change, others do too. So, it's inevitable that our friends will flow in and out of our lives, growing and changing as we do.

And yet, there's nothing quite as cutting as the end of a friendship. We ghost our friend instead of saying goodbye to them. We talk about them to others instead of being honest to their face. We resent them instead of thanking them. If only we were taught in school how to navigate relationships. If only we knew the importance of honoring what once was and how to complete in peace.

The end of a friendship can leave us in an undefined area. While the boundaries of a romantic relationship are generally distinct, those of a friendship are more blurred, which can lead to confusion and second guessing. When a significant friendship in our life ends it's so important to honor that ending, and yet in our society, we don't have rituals to support this.

The most painful relationship endings I've experienced have been those with friends. It's only happened a couple of times, yet the feelings ran deep. And the pain primarily came from a lack of communication around the ending itself and the honoring of the beauty that the relationship brought for the seasons of our lives. Avoidance brews confusion, which creates an open ending instead of a clean slate.

## SOUL INQUIRY

*Have friendships ended in your life that you haven't been given the space to mourn?*

*Is there anything you're being called to do to honor this ending?*

# △
# LET IT BREAK YOU TO REMAKE YOU

Let it break you to remake you. Don't close down. Don't shut off. The only way to move from the tomb of who we once were to the womb of who we soon will be is to stay in it. To stay open to it and through it. To trust the fertile darkness of the void of new beginnings. Through the separation of the only thing you knew. Through the uncertainty of your becoming.

The day you were born was your first initiation and it holds within it the codes of your forever becoming. The quickest way for transformation to occur is to find a way to open to it and through it. This is the challenge of all rebirths. To somehow find the breath of Life and let it move through us, no matter how intense the contractions.

Any midwife knows that it's at the heightened moment of transition that the initiate most doubts their ability to cross the threshold and be born anew. To go from one state to the next. It's when we're standing at the edge and are invited to leap into the abyss that we most want to back up and pack up. To shut down. To close. To go unconscious. To cling on to anything that will ease the pain. To make it go away. To control and contain the incomprehensible power of Life.

The midwife also knows that it's in the moment when we're certain we can't make it to the other side, that we're about to transition through it. That we've never been closer to our transformation than when we think we can't possibly go on. But for the transformation to happen, we need to be willing to let it break us (change us) in order for it to remake us (transform us). To shatter the shackles that are keeping us bound to who we once were for the chance to be born anew. This is what it is to truly live.

Yes, it's at the most impossible moment that the rebirth actually occurs. And that's not only a miracle but also a fundamental law of nature, the cosmos, and planet Earth. Your cells know it. Your soul does too. It's your head that needs reminding. We are all being invited to birth ourselves anew.

And so, the only way to move from the tomb of who we once were to the womb of who we soon will be is to give in to the birthing energy, to the breath of life energy, and find a way to open to it and through it. To let the throes of labor break you so they can remake you. These are the birth mysteries.

## SOUL INQUIRY

*Which part of you are you being called to*
*surrender in order to be born anew?*

# ▲
# RELEASING THE PETALS OF THE PAST

When an ending occurs, there comes a point when we can't go back. In a seemingly fleeting moment, the road that led us here is suddenly impossible to access. There's a sinking knowing that things will never be the same again.

A death, a birth, a loss, a growth, an ending, a discovery. No matter how hard you try, things are different now. You're different now. The world's different now. What's been seen can't be unseen. Something new beckons you forth. Courage is required for the rebirth to happen. The rose hip knows, the phoenix does too, that we need to surrender what was to the Earth, to one day be transformed anew.

We can cling on to the petals of the past as the winds of change blow. But eventually, we'll discover that change is coming, change is near, change is already here. And while what once was is no longer and what soon will be is not yet, it's time to offer what once was to the soil and let it nourish the seeds deep within. Had the clouds not released the water they were holding, the trees would not have received the nourishment they needed to grow. When we gather up the courage to release what was, we're greeted by the fruits of our sweetest future.

## SOUL INQUIRY

*What are you being called to let go of?*

*If you weren't afraid of change, what would you embrace?*

# the fertile void of her becoming

She built her house with sticks and stones.
Urgently, just like she'd been shown.
On ground that was never actually hers to own.
In a place that was chosen for her, not by her.

What she thought was the earth was in fact a
ledge. Forever crumbling. Her stable unstable.

The higher she built, the further the fall.
The inevitable winds of change a constant threat.

So many moments of unbridled joy wasted
worrying about a million possible
distant futures and pasts.
None of which were actually hers in the first place.

Haunted by a hypervigilance that told her
it was never safe to rest.
Run by the thing she was so
desperately attempting to run from.

Frozen by stories inherited. Her soul would wake her in
the dark of night, the tower burning.

Her body a volcano of ancient intergenerational rage.
Dormant for centuries and now readied to erupt.

For nine months her body became earth for another.
From cells to organs, bones to flesh.
She was home for a soul to plant itself here.
A portal for spirit to descend into matter.

It made her realize how much
she longed to descend herself.
Into the sureness of the deep, dark,
damp soil of the Goddess.

So she stopped reaching and instead made her
descent into the muddy Earth that was always
available to hold her.
And sank deep into the fertile void of her becoming.

# △
# THE SECOND BLOOM

Just when we think the summer season's over and autumn's drawing near, some flowers bless us with an unexpected second bloom. Perhaps you have a creation that's waiting to be brought forth, or a new relationship or passion in your life. Maybe what's waiting to be born is a new version of you.

The more open we are to change, the more open we are to Life. The more open we are to Life, the more open we are to being born anew. Yes, this is what it means to truly live. Being open to saying yes to Life – so when you eventually take your last breath, you'll exhale with no dreams left unlived within you.

It's never too late to surrender to what's blooming within you. All that matters is that you trust the buds that are longing to grow and be known. Regardless of your age or what may have previously occurred, you're being called to surrender to a second bloom. To welcome the new and share it with the world. To acknowledge your secret passions, longings, creations, and yearnings and let them flower and fruit.

If we properly allow things to end, new beginnings will always come. If we surrender to the cycles of life, after winter, spring will always return. If we tend the seeds in the fertile earth, they'll eventually emerge.

## SOUL INQUIRY

*What unexpected or secret dream wants*
*to flower and fruit within you?*

It took getting to the middle of her life
for her to realize that the thing
she was running from
was actually running her.

*burned out* △

# △
# WE'RE ALL RUNNING
# FROM SOMETHING

Sometimes it takes stopping for you to realize the pace you've been going and how long you've been running.

Sometimes it takes your world to crumble for you to realize that the very thing you've been running from has been running you.

Sometimes it takes being forced to slow down for you to realize that the only way to stop is to face it.

Sometimes it takes your worst fears to be realized for you to slow down and truly live.

We're all running from something.

What's running you?

## SOUL INQUIRY

*What are you running from?*

*What is running you?*

# △
# WHAT ARE YOU REALLY LONGING FOR?

Regulate to the pace of the Earth. Slow down to that intelligent, rhythmic pulse. It's been beating since the Earth was young, well before the first Mother had come. Find your way back to its hypnotic rhythm. You'll find peace there. Rest, rejuvenation, and inspiration aplenty too. You'll uncover the codes of creation and the blueprint for why you chose to come.

It's true what they say – everything your soul is seeking is also seeking you. Stop the endless searching in places different to where you are. Your soul is always calling you toward it and it speaks in yearnings and longings. The four chambers of your heart are all you need to locate the golden thread of your life. After that comes the courage needed to walk it into the bones and flesh of your life. This is a planet of manifestation, yes, but all the searching and reaching will only ever leave you weary and hungrier than before. For there's a difference between co-creating and accumulating. Choose to co-create and your destiny will become your fate.

All that you co-create cannot be taken from you, for creativity is given to you in the moment. The satisfaction can be felt as you merge with Life to birth something new. The life-force increases within you, and you too are brought back to life. And when you're there at the end of your days, it's the love you've given, the hearts you've cradled, and what you've uniquely created that will have you knowing just how fully you've been living.

## SOUL INQUIRY

*What is your soul really yearning and longing for?*

# a hundred different people

I've already been a hundred different people.
And I know I'll be a hundred more.
I'm tired of pretending to the world that
I still am who I thought I was.

With so many people thinking they
know me and telling me who they
think I am, it's hard to know myself.

Of course I'm not who they thought I was.
I'm not who I thought I was before either.
Right now, in this moment,
I've already changed.

In an age where we curate who
we are for strangers on the internet,

it's easy to feel masked
and trapped.

The only way to know yourself
is to realize that the moment
you think you know yourself,
you must let that go, because by then
you'll have changed into someone else.

If someone tells you:
'You've changed...'
say, 'Of course, naturally!'

I've already been a hundred different people.
And one day soon,
I'm sure I'll be a hundred more.

# △
# SET YOUR SOUL FREE

When you repeatedly project an image of who you are onto the world, it takes a toll on the soul. For the soul is part of the great mystery. It's impossible to contain it or fit it into a neat little box. And it yearns to feel free above all else. The projections of others tug heavily on the soul, and this can cause us to create a wall around our heart to protect it. But the moment those walls are erected, the soul longs for room to breathe.

Don't box yourself in. Remove the fences, the overscheduling, and the need for perfection and give your soul space to be. Your soul needs room to feel free. It's multidimensional, never just one thing. It's not possible just to be one thing. If you try, you'll find yourself in a cage of your own creation. The moment you feel trapped, captive, you cut yourself off from spirit and creativity. The soul longs to co-create with Life.

So, free yourself of anything that attempts to define you or confine you. Leap into the unknown and give your soul space to dream. Gather the courage to embrace the great mystery of you as an ever-changing expression of spirit woven into matter. Set your soul and your creative spirit free.

## SOUL INQUIRY

*What's making you feel trapped right now?*

*What are you being called to do to feel more free?*

# the cage of a consciously created life

When she first woke up,
she created a new story for herself.
No, more than that: she created a whole new life.

One that felt congruent with who she was,
not who she'd been raised by the world to be.
One that felt like it could hold her multidimensionality.

But then, life changed, the world changed.
And right alongside it, so did she.

And once again she woke up in the middle of a life that
she'd consciously created but which no longer fitted
who she was and who she was called to be.

She longed so much to free herself
from the shackles of her dreams fulfilled.

She yearned not for a life
different to the one she was in.
But the space to be who she was becoming, in it.

△

# SELF-ABANDONMENT

People are meant to change and so it's normal that relationships do too. Change is hard to navigate, but it hurts so much more deeply when we make our worth and happiness dependent on external things and people. We may have learned that abandoning ourselves is the only way to prevent others abandoning us. It hurts when someone abandons us, but it hurts 10 times more if we abandon ourselves by being who we *think* they want us to be and still they abandon us.

When the fear of abandonment comes up, the invitation is always to turn toward yourself and say, I'll never leave you. To offer yourself the love and companionship you're afraid of losing or not receiving. To find safety in your own company. To find love in your own presence.

We can choose never to leave ourselves. To be loyal, compassionate protectors of the precious one who chose to be here in this body, on this planet, at this time. You're your most reliable companion. And while this practice may not have been modeled for you when you were young, you can cultivate it and make this commitment now. Invite your adult self to turn to your child self and say: No matter what happens, I'll never leave your side. No matter what happens, I'll never, ever abandon you.

## SOUL INQUIRY

*How do you abandon yourself or have you*
*abandoned yourself in the past?*

*What can you do differently to choose yourself?*

△
# BEING LOVED FOR WHO YOU ARE, NOT WHAT YOU ARE

Being understood is a human need. During our early years, being loved for *who* we are rather than *what* we are can set the trajectory of our lives. It allows self-love and self-belief to develop. When we're misunderstood or loved only for what we are, we believe that we must perform to receive the love that's our birthright. Being ourselves isn't enough. And this causes more pain than it's worth.

It's possible to heal and receive this love and understanding as an adult, but it requires us to feel the sorrow, rage, or hurt and then take the child within into our hearts and give ourselves what we didn't receive at the time. Sometimes, it's this sort of separation that leads people down a spiritual path, inspiring a deeper searching and yearning for a love not yet received but deeply longed for, even remembered by the soul. This longing sends us on a quest to find it. An unconditional holding. A yearning to fall into the arms of the Great Mother.

So much has been severed in our society that we yearn for the ancient connection with the Earth, and it's all coming up now to be healed. It's being purged from within so many of us. So many are processing what until now has not been safe to feel; perhaps this is part of the great healing and rebirth. Ancient and future ancestors call us back and forth to mend what's been severed. Each of us who has the courage to feel is clearing a little bit in our lineage. And in doing so, slowly but surely, we're finding our way back to ourselves, each other, and the Earth.

## SOUL INQUIRY

*Whose love are you longing for and how could you devote that energy to yourself?*

She looked into her own eyes
and instructed her soul not to leave.
She knew that shame was a tool used by the patriarchy.
And this time, she refused to be anything
but wild, unbound and free.

*soul retrieval* △

△

# THERE'S NOTHING WRONG WITH YOU

You're holy and whole. You're innocent and innately good. You didn't get kicked out of the garden. None of us did. You're wholly welcome here. If you feel as if you've done something wrong without knowing what it is; if you feel ashamed about hurting someone, or if you're finding it hard to forgive yourself, it's time to release any shame, judgment, or bad feelings. To do what you need to do to let go and make amends. To remember that you're human. And as a human you're here to learn and grow. And so is everyone else.

There's nothing wrong with you. You're an ever-changing work in progress. We all are. You're learning and unlearning. We all are. Be gentle with yourself and in turn be gentle with others. Return to your humanity. Your humanness.

Remember that you were never perfect and being human isn't about perfection. Grow and learn – but do it softly. You have a right to be here because you *are* here. You don't need to prove your worth. You have goodness in you. Remember that. Cherish that. And cherish that in others too.

We're all doing the best we can. When we learn, we can choose to do something new. Commit to learning and doing better each and every day. This is what it means to be human. To embrace our humanness. Without it, we deny our shadow, and it's through facing the shadow without defenses that we can learn and grow. Embrace your humanity and you'll find it easier to embrace others and the whole world. Lay down your sword – you've nothing left to prove.

## SOUL INQUIRY

*How can you be gentler with yourself?*

For the first time,
she looked in the mirror
and saw herself as she really was.

A cosmic miracle experiencing
herself in the physical.

*the temple is you* △

# △
# THE UNSEEN LAYERS OF HEALING

There are so many layers to healing, especially when we're healing within a system or a relationship. Patterns passed down and ruptures left unacknowledged – don't underestimate the number of layers and threads of healing.

Sometimes, you can find yourself in a constellation or a system in which no matter how hard you try, the work of others is required for the healing to happen. Try to soften when you feel frustrated about not being past what came from your past. There's often much more to the healing than just you. If you find yourself holding the threads of healing within a system that has no interest in healing itself, and you've given it your all, it's okay to stop trying to do it in the physical and to shift into the spiritual. For doing it in the physical isn't always possible.

There are many layers to healing and not just in ourselves. Ancestrally, we hold it in our bodies, in our cells, and in the beliefs, stories, traumas, and wounds of those who came before us. Of course, we carry the gifts, strengths, and triumphs too.

When one heals in the family system, it sends ripples down the ancestral line, all the way forward and all the way back. If you have others willing to heal in your system, they'll be a helpful cog, turning in the healing of the line, and in turn, the healing of humanity. Those who chose to come to lineages filled with ones who unconsciously cling to the wounds instead of consciously embracing the healing of the line have signed up to a bigger task.

Call upon allies from your lineage, all the way back and all the way forward, to help you now in the present. You don't need to do this alone, even if, in the physical, it seems as though you are doing it alone. Don't beat yourself up and think that there's something wrong with you because you feel too much in a lineage that's repressed so much. If you feel too much, chances are you have a huge capacity to love and feel, for grief is evidence of how much you love and how open your heart is.

Remember, every moment of every day, healing is happening. It's brave to keep your heart open when others in your system direct their pain onto you.

## SOUL INQUIRY

*How can you be more patient and tender toward yourself?*

# individuation

After hungry years looking to others
to give and receive the love she came in with,
she decided instead to redirect it to herself.

She unhooked herself from the system
that had her reaching for something
she could never, ever get.

After decades spent waiting,
she took her place as an elder
when those elder than her had not,
because those elder than them had not.

She initiated herself so that one day
she could initiate someone else.

# △
# THE ONE WHO HAS THE
# COURAGE TO HEAL

Some of us are here to feel what's not been felt. To process what's not been processed. To heal on behalf of those who could not. Healing is change. Perpetual. Healing isn't easy. Healing isn't pretty. It takes great courage to heal. You cannot awaken without it. And it's also the most natural thing in the world.

Ancestral patterns and memories are spiraling within us. Many are experiencing a sudden processing of things lived and passed down from cell to cell. As a planet, we're hurtling back to the earth of our bodies and to our humanity. Being urged to return to the arms of each other. To be the mother and father we most long for. To be the home we most long for. To return to the Earth, to our bodies, to each other.

Pain travels through societies and ancestral lines until someone is awake, open-hearted, and brave enough to feel it. This is the role of the healer in the system, the cycle breaker: to remind the courageous one who refuses to close off their heart to the world that they are not their pain, and that healing is always happening, every moment of every day.

*We can all be healers if we choose it.*
*For healing is change and change is*
*nature, and nature is in our DNA.*

The ancestral line is the first system we're born into. The healer in the system, the cycle breaker, feels the things others could not. They're here to process what until now has not been safe to feel and heal. It's disorientating, and some of the deepest healing work there is. The healer energetically takes on and processes what others in the system have cut off from: anger, pain, grief, despair, sorrow, guilt, regret, shame. The healer is often thought of as a problem to fix rather than the one who's revealing what's broken in the system. In a healthy society, those who are hurting are embraced rather than isolated and made wrong or right.

In my shamanic training I learned about the energetic impact that family secrets have on the well-being of members of a family line. A family secret is events or information that members hide from each other or those outside the family. I don't know any family line that doesn't have one of these. And we're living in a time when so many secrets are coming into the light within so many different systems of the world.

The system will either consciously or subconsciously prevent the secret from getting out. And so the healer, the one who has taken on processing it, is left even more isolated and misunderstood. The healer is freed when they understand the energy they have taken on and give it back to its rightful owner. The entire system is then freed if the rightful owner gathers up the courage to acknowledge what they have been avoiding feeling from the beginning. But it's possible to do it on their behalf too.

## SOUL INQUIRY

*What ancestral pattern are you being called to clear?*

*Are there systems that you came here to heal or shift?*

*Does your family have a secret that you know of?*

It's much easier to blame a person than a system.
When you blame a person,
the problem is external and fixed.

Burn the 'other.'
Silence the truth speaker.
Drown the dreamer.
Throw the disrupter under the bus.

When you blame a system you then
need to face the part you played in it.
It's much easier to blame a person than a system.

*cycle breaker* △

# △
# THE CYCLE BREAKERS

Cycle breakers are here to activate something within a system. But to do so, they first bring up within others what's yet to be healed, for nothing can be healed until it's felt.

Not everyone wants to heal – healing means facing pain and so many choose to push it away. If you're a cycle breaker, the thing you need to realize is that your presence activates and heals, but it may not always be received or perceived accurately. Try your best not to take it personally. As a conscious dreamer, you were born to change things. To not think and act like everyone else. To live a new waking dream. You were never meant to fit in, to be the same. You came here to change things.

The wildflowers and the weeds know. The animals do too. Diversity is crucial for the harmony of the Earth. Don't spend your time trying to be anything other than what you are. Those who try to change you fear uncertainty and are most likely uncomfortable in your presence. But it's your presence that's healing.

*Keep being present to your soul's dreaming. You're here to process what's not been processed. To activate things within your system that are ready to be healed.*

But to heal it, you need to feel it, and feeling it takes grit and guts. To heal something, you first must acknowledge what's broken or frozen. You're here to breathe life into the parts of the system that have been separated or frozen. Where spirit and matter have been split. This isn't easy. But you knew that coming in. And while some of you may feel as if you're doing this work alone, please know that you are part of a much wider team of souls who said yes to the collective healing of humanity.

You're all strategically placed in all corners of the planet. Know that even if you feel alone in the physical, in the spiritual there are many more souls right alongside you. Call upon their support and encouragement when you most need it and send yours to them.

I know this life can feel confusing and I know how lonely it can get. But rest assured that it can be filled with such sweet joy too. So often, the antidote to that which hurts us is to face it completely. Your life-force is precious. If you spend your life avoiding, you'll also avoid the present moment. And the present moment is the only place you can realize the waking dream of your soul, which is to fully live.

We're the cycle-breaking generations. Here to bring a huge realignment. May we do it with kindness.

## SOUL INQUIRY

*Can you think of anyone in your life who plays the role of cycle breaker within a system? (And it can be you.)*

*How can you extend your compassion and support to them?*

I call upon helpful, positive ancestors
of future, present, and past.

Free us from these unconscious
patterns that are harming us all.
Free us from these patterns
in a way that truly lasts.

**May we be unbound,
unbound, forever unbound.**

# △
# MOTHER, OUR FIRST LOVE

*'It's often said that the first sound we hear in the
womb is our mother's heartbeat... We vibrate to that
primordial rhythm even before we have ears to hear.'*

LAYNE REDMOND

The love we have for our mother is like no other. It's the first sensual and intimate relationship we have. The love we have for our mother influences all the relationships that come after. She's the portal through which we come into this world. The gateway and giver of life.

Regardless of how we were raised, the first relationship we have before we enter this world is with our biological mother. We gestate in the watery world of her cells, her DNA, her emotions, her beliefs, her love, her thoughts, her joy, her grief, her tears, and her fears – her all is imprinted onto us.

Who our mother is affects who we will be. And the same went for her mother and her mother's mother. On and on it goes, all the way back to the Great Mother. From cell to organ, flesh to body, Mother gives us life. Mother sustains us. Mother is our first world – the only one we know until we cross the threshold from water to air and Earth as we learn to breathe on our own at the moment of separation.

Our relationship with the archetype of Mother reveals our relationship with our body and the Earth. Our relationship with the archetype of Mother is far deeper than that we have with the person who gestated us or raised us, the one who was present or wasn't. Our relationship with the archetype of Mother encapsulates our relationship with Life itself.

Our relationship with the archetype of Mother brings up the truth of how disconnected from the feminine our society has become. Our relationship with the archetype of Mother shines a light on how impossible it is for anyone to live up to the archetype of Mother in a patriarchal world. How all mothers are set up to fail.

What we learn and believe about the archetype of Mother influences how we mother and care for others and ourselves. And regardless of our life experience, with consciousness, we get to choose how we do that. If we haven't had a positive modeling or understanding of this archetype, we can choose to find a way to redefine and envision this for ourselves.

## SOUL INQUIRY

*What did/do you most yearn for from your mother?*

*What did/does your mother most yearn for?*

*How can you be a loving mother to yourself?*

△

# HEALING THE MOTHER LINE

During my mystical experience with the Great Mother at the center of the Earth, and in my subsequent research into intergenerational trauma and mother line healing, I discovered that at a cellular level, we each spent five months inside the womb of our grandmother, and that she in turn formed within the womb of *her* grandmother. On and on it goes, back down the mother line for us all. And therein lies the opportunity for us to play our part in the healing of humanity.

Through our mother line we can clear what's been severed. Through our mother line we can reach all the way back to the Original Mother. You can do this work without being in contact with your biological mother, and whether she is living or dead. Through our mother line we can return to each other. Healing the mother line can begin with healing the relationship you have with your own mother; however, you'll soon realize that it's not all about her. She was the body in which you grew and the portal through which your soul chose to enter at this time.

She may have been the one in which you felt the agony of separation for the first time, for as I've said, our mother is our first great love as we were at one point one with her. However, if you dig a little deeper, you'll find a trail leading back to the center point of humanity through the mother line. And there, passed down from cell to cell, are all the crimes against the feminine and humanity.

This is a time of much unwinding and unbinding, of mourning and healing, of humble acceptance and deep cellular processing. What's previously been overlooked, misunderstood, pushed down, glossed over, and bypassed is erupting from deep within us and all around us. We're seeing what's been stored in the cells that existed before we even chose to come. The moments when the soul and cell were separated. Memories imprinted to us and through us. The processing of things lived but not felt, transmitted from cell to cell, body to body, generation to generation until there's consciousness, safety, space, and an urgency to feel it.

Those who are the courageous containers to do this processing, this feeling, this healing – the cycle breakers, the healers in the system – are so often misunderstood. Seen as weak, volatile, and unstable rather than courageous, open, and holy. We're hurtling back to the Earth, to the Earth, to the Earth. Body. Matter. Mother. Urged to slow down to her pace. To return to the arms of each other. Humbled. Awed. Human. Healing on behalf of those who could not.

We're living through in-between times. Rebirthing times. Transfiguration times. Sometimes a soul is born into a system to heal it. But to heal it they must go to the places where those who shut down and cut off could not. Collectively, we're facing the harm that colonialism, patriarchy, and toxic capitalism have imprinted on us, especially with regard to the feminine. So many born to mothers who were born to mothers who were born to mothers who were not respected, protected, supported, and revered themselves. It's time to mend the chain. And it's not only about the feminine rising. Union is what we really desire.

Send healing to your mother line with the Unbound chant (*see page xiii*).

## SOUL INQUIRY

*What strengths did you inherit from your mother line?*

*What pattern/s do you want to free yourself from?*

*How are you being called to send healing to your mother line and set yourself and all of the mothers free?*

I reach all the way
back to the Original Mother,
and I set all the mothers,
and myself, free.

*healing the mother line* △

# △
# THE POWER OF ANGER: CREATION OR DESTRUCTION

We tend to see anger and rage as emotions to control or restrain. And expressing them as less than ideal or even bad. Boys are taught that their anger is dangerous and women that their rage isn't feminine. Women who have the courage to harness their anger are often accused of being crazy and unstable, and this threat then stops them from cultivating their power in the flames of their sacred rage. It halts the flow of passion and the ferocious urge for the feminine to protect what's sacred. (Of course, the feminine exists within all people, regardless of gender.)

Our anger and rage are often a reflection of what's important to us. They can be a signpost to our boundaries, or lack thereof, and a guiding light revealing what we truly care about, long for, or wish to protect. They can also hold within them the codes of our true purpose. However, we must do the job of listening to our anger and rage and offering them a safe space to be released and expressed.

When we repress an emotion, there's always a consequence; it might fester in the body and make us sick; it might paralyze us and prevent us from living passionately; or it might come out in ways that are physically, mentally, and emotionally harmful to others. I believe that like anything and anyone, our anger softens when it's witnessed. I'm mindful that often this isn't straightforward when we're in the midst of experiencing it, but as with all things on the spiritual path, doing the work to turn inward and listen deeply reveals the wisdom and insight that can cultivate positive change.

**When we understand our relationship with our emotions – especially the big ones like anger and rage – and let them be expressed safely, we're able to be healthier beings who cause less harm in the world.**

When it comes to expressing anger and rage, I find it's about releasing and transmuting them in ways that are safe, positive, healthy, and life-affirming. Safe doesn't necessarily mean quiet, but it does mean conscious. I'll never forget the time my husband became very angry about something and expressed it in a very raw way. I called my friend Binnie and told her about it, expecting her to agree that his behavior was unacceptable. But her response shocked me.

'How wonderful that he was able to express that so freely, and in such a safe way,' she said. 'Many people hold it in and then it comes out in harmful ways or transforms into deep grief and sadness. You know, I believe that anger is really all our passion, all our life energy that's been held back because it has a negative thought attached. Which is almost always, I'm helpless, hopeless, or powerless to do anything about it... Yep, that's anger – PASSION.'

Binnie's words flipped my understanding of this force within us. Anger is a strong emotion that can be deeply sacred and holy. Anger delivers clear information, and it can be used to create incredible things in the world. If we're consciously living, the invitation is to try to understand that and embrace the energy and express it consciously. For example, if you're outraged about something that's happening in the world or to you, think about how you can use this energy to create rather than destroy.

Anger can indicate that you're passionate about something – that there's a fire within you that's been ignited. So, how can you direct this energy in a sacred way? How can you use this energy to create something new rather than perpetuate harm? How can you harness the power of the fire within rather than burning everything down?

Repressed anger can also stagnate in the body as grief. I experienced this firsthand many years ago while in the early stages of recovering from the end of a long-term relationship to which I'd given everything. The breakup had been amicable, but I was struggling to move on. It took finding out that my former partner was in a new relationship for the unrepressed anger to be released. Years and years of pushing it down had left me frozen and stuck, but this news invited it to bubble up.

A therapist friend suggested I find a way to safely express what was erupting inside me, and together we came up with a plan. After collecting some glass jars from the fridge, I went into the little courtyard garden of my studio apartment, lay a large sheet on the ground, took a deep breath and, harnessing all the energy within me, I threw the jars against the stone wall. I let out a loud scream after each smash, with the intention of fully releasing the anger, and I kept going until it felt complete.

Next, I created a playlist of high-energy songs and for 21 days I did a dance practice in which for one song I'd shake out any sadness or anger from my body and for another I'd dance it out too – allowing my body to move in any way it needed to. I felt liberated, inspired, free, and more alive than I had for almost a decade. Soon after, I gathered the courage to put on my first workshop – something I'd been called to do for many years but had avoided because of fear. Moving the energy out of my body in a safe way seemed to shift the sadness and fear in it.

Now, more than ever, we need to embrace what *is* and alchemize it rather than bypass it because we think it's not spiritual to do so or it may make us or others feel uncomfortable. If you ask me, alchemizing anger in positive ways, and using it to CREATE rather than repress or negatively destroy, is some of the holiest work there is!

## SOUL INQUIRY

*What do you feel angry or frustrated about?*

*What is the anger or frustration trying to tell you? What does it want you to know?*

*In what ways do you feel helpless, hopeless, or powerless? Can you think of a positive way that you can move and use this energy that's in your body?*

*How can you transform your anger into passion (moving from what you're against to what you're for)?*

# △
# THE TIMES OF INTEGRATION
# AND HEALING

Some souls are born in places with people who cannot see the soul who has landed, and as a result, they may long for a sacred recognition, an acknowledgment of their great entrance Earth-side, that never comes. However, in most cases, this isn't a conscious act: how can someone recognize the sacred in another when it wasn't recognized in them?

It takes a lot to change this. And yet, this lack of recognition may be the fuel that's necessary to send the soul on a search to meet this ache. At first, they'll reach out to the world, asking it to see them. And they may find some who, upon meeting them, do see them. But ultimately, they'll learn that they can always recognize the sacred in themselves. And recognizing the sacred in themselves makes it easier for others to recognize it in them too.

Increasing numbers of souls have chosen to incarnate in ancestries and lands different from before. This simple change has been disrupting the patterns and awakening dormant energy within family systems. Coming into a line that's entrenched in old ways of being isn't straightforward or easy. It can lead a soul to feel misunderstood and misplaced. But if you did come in, if you're here reading this, know that it's one of the ways that so much healing and change is now possible.

In times like these, so much that would otherwise have remained dormant is dislodging and beginning to shift. The foundations of the way things were are trembling beneath your feet. Ancestors past are freed through your liberation. Ancestors future are cheering you on. There's a new way forward for humanity.

A new way of realigning ourselves with the pure and potent pulse of Life. We're remembering the ancient ways of the Earth and we're dreaming a new Earth in too. Right now. You're doing it. Just by living your waking dream. The times of integration and healing are here.

## SOUL INQUIRY

*Whose acknowledgment are you longing for?*

*How can you give this to yourself now?*

# △
# RETURNING TO OURSELVES
# AND EACH OTHER

The more you take, the emptier you'll feel. The more you've been severed, the more severing you'll be programmed to do. The more invaded your space has become, the more likely you are to want to grab and take back. It takes consciousness, courage, an open heart and a sober soul to choose to break the chain of suffering inherited.

We're all walking the labyrinth in search of the center of a healed self and a healed humanity. And when we finally get there, to the center, we have a choice: to retrace the steps of what's been walked before us or done to us or to let ourselves be unwound and unbound by the Spirit of Life. To be the weavers of a healed humanity. To find some way in which, instead of doing what's been done to us or before us, we choose to birth this world anew.

Flowers don't open and close according to who's walking by: they reveal their beauty to the world without waver. You're here to do that too. There are people who at a soul level chose to walk alongside you. But if they're to find you, you must first let them see you. Reveal yourself to the world. Open your heart and mind to collaboration rather than competition.

So many of us, particularly those who identify as women, have learned to be mistrustful of one another, as if we're competing. We were never meant to walk this life alone. We came here in waves. It's time to come back together. To remember that we're not in competition; instead, we hold keys for each other. Maybe this has its roots in the societies of the Middle Ages, a time when we were positioned against one another. When our power was seen as something to be feared. Or maybe it began long before that.

The feminine has risen. There's further for her to go, but she's here. The days of mistrusting others, of ultra-independence, are coming to an end. Unhook yourself from the systems and ways of being that position you in competition with others. We came here in teams, and we're part of the same living dream. Choose co-creating over conquering.

## RETURNING TO OURSELVES AND EACH OTHER ACTIVATION

*I release any old programming of competition. I open myself up to relationships and collaborations. It's safe for me to trust and co-create.*

# △
# WE CAME HERE FOR THIS

*'Individuation begins with the painful
recognition that we're all orphans.
And the liberating recognition that the
whole world is our orphanage.'*

MARION WOODMAN

We're living in times of crumbling. All that we've put on a pedestal is falling, perhaps so that we can realize that we're *all* sacred and holy. The tower is burning, and the walls between us must come down.

These are times of rebuilding, but first comes the fall. All the ways in which we and society have put structures, systems, people, and all other living beings either above or below – as something to own, cage, conquer, control – are coming to a halt. It's painful. And it's necessary. We all have a part to play as the planets do their sacred dance.

Some are here to tear down; some are here to mend. Some are here to reimagine; some are here to plant and pray. Some are here to birth anew; some are here to tend the wounds. May we find a way back to each other, even if at first a separation is required. May we find a way to extend our hearts, especially when we're bruised and tender. May we find a way to heal what feels hopeless and broken. May we find a way back to each other. True healing can only happen when we allow ourselves to do that.

By acknowledging the history of the Earth beneath us in times and consciousnesses different to those today, we can begin to face what's been severed and open the pathways of healing. Regardless of whether it was done by us, to us, or well before us. When we acknowledge it, we begin to clear and reactivate our connection with it. To shake the inherited need to conquer, take, control, or own in a bid to feel as if we're important, when deep down all we yearn for is to know that we belong.

We're the new keepers of the Earth. Future ancestors. Current custodians. Inheritors of the bad and the good. May we find the courage to mend what's been broken.

## SOUL INQUIRY

*What difficult thing are you being called to admit or face?*

## △
# LET YOUR SOUL STIR

You're being called to change the way you see the world and the dynamics within the systems and constellations in which you find yourself. We need lights in all parts of society. Don't run from where you are; stand tall and emanate. It's difficult being the light in dark times such as these, but never before have there been more of us awake and on mission. You came in knowing what to do. Your blueprint is seeded within.

Each night that you go to sleep and then wake up you're remembering more and more of your soul's dream. You're the waking dream that your soul came here to live. Your body, your place of incarnation, your ancestry are vessels for the unique frequency your soul came here to embody. It doesn't matter how you express it, only that you do.

*Your presence here on this planet, at this time, isn't a fluke. Your soul not only chose to be here, it also dreamed it.*

Your mind could never fathom the intricate details of your soul's plan. Which is why it's so important that you do what you can to tend the relationship you have with the wise one within. Your soul has within it the map to the life it came here to live. It's available to guide you every moment of every day. All you need to do is spend time with it. This isn't a one-time thing. It's a forever dance.

One day soon the world will see what you can sense and feel right now. I know it's difficult to live a waking dream in a world in which so many are still asleep, but as more and more wake up – and they are and will continue to do so – the dream becomes more and more real. And you living your waking dream will cause others to stir from their slumber. You came here as a visionary, conscious dreamer, a seed for the future garden of the Earth. Your presence has the power to activate, awaken, and bless.

Think less about getting it right or wrong and more about embodying, living your soul's dream, and emanating. You're a blessed thread in the tapestry of a new humanity. Not everyone sees what you see, which is why holding your vision is itself visionary. Not everyone is awake to their soul's dream. Do your best to shed your fear, your need to fit in and get it right. Your path is different from any other, which is why your navigation must come from within. Your being here matters. Especially now.

## SOUL INQUIRY

*What is your soul's secret dream?*

# the waking dream

There will come a time when the mysteries
of today will be clear and understood.

When the many threads will be
woven into a tapestry complete, and
we will see beyond this single thread.

When we'll wake up from our slumber and
find ourselves as the ordered Universe,
living a waking dream.

# △
# THE QUICKENING

A message from the Ancient Grandmothers of the Earth:

We're the guardians of humanity and the connection with the ancient Earth. We're here to assist you in healing your ancestral lines all the way back and all the way forward. You hold the thread to your healing, and we speak to you through these threads. We know that it's difficult to gain perspective on this healing process – that when you're in it, you can struggle to see the greater whole. But know that we stand beside you and all around you, forever singing you on.

You're playing an instrumental role in the healing of humanity. Every person on the planet is. This time is one of great integration, clearing, and momentum. This healing process has been building since long before your lifetime. Yet things are speeding up. We call it the quickening. All that you do now has a deep ripple effect on the world of humanity. All that you do now will be felt far and wide, although you may not see the direct results in your lifetime.

There are energies at play that will try to distract and confuse you. It's time now to anchor more deeply into the heart. In the heart, no external energetic force can find you. In the heart, you'll hear us more clearly.

Your congruence and presence have the potential to heal in ways that you might not yet see. As each person finds their soul's resonance, humanity's healing is made more possible. You're each a cell in the organism of humanity. As each cell is activated it leads others to attune and activate too. To align with the life-force within all living things at its highest. This is what it means to harmonize.

The trauma that's coming up isn't yours alone. It's both ancestral and collective. There are some who have come here to process on behalf of their ancestry. Others, for the collective. Many are doing both. To choose this path is a courageous thing for the soul. If it's been part of yours, know that if your soul chose it, then you can survive it. And when you do, you'll not just survive, you'll thrive.

Right now, it may be difficult and confusing. Stay connected to the light and with the positive ones from your ancestry, the ones who never forgot. Call upon them and others to support you. You'll likely need a multifaceted support system because what you're processing and clearing is multifaceted too. There are so many layers. Call it all in from both the seen and unseen worlds around you.

You can survive this and one day soon you'll be thriving. This is our vision for you. And for the entire Earth. The deeper you go, the more you can hold others in too. This is the dawn of a new way for you. This is the dawn of a new way for your ancestry. This is the dawn of a new way for humanity. Trust the healing thread you're holding.

# i forget, I remember, I forget, I re-remember

Sometimes there are moments when
I question being here in these times.
Perhaps I made a big mistake and chose the
wrong body, the wrong planet, the wrong time.

The push–pull of polarity.
The starvation of sacred in our culture.
The division and the ancestral trauma that
feel too much for me to process.
The difficulty of individuation.
The agonizing ecstasy of life on this
glorious mystical planet.

The tragic messy beauty of being human.
Soul embodied. Spirit planted.
Light seeded into matter.

The ever-changing way of things as we
spin our way through space and time in
suits of cell, star, skin, and flesh.
But then the flowers open.

And the birds sing.
The trees reach.
The land leads.
The stones speak.

And a fellow traveler recognizes me
the moment we first meet.
And over and over, and again and again
I forget and then I re-remember
who I am and why I chose to come.

I remember that I'm the flower.
I'm the tree. The land is me.
I'm the bird. I'm the stones. I'm the ocean.
The other is me.
Recognizing this sets us both free.

And over and over, and again and again
I remember, I forget, and then
I re-remember who I am and
why I chose to come.

Part Three

# THE WAY
## *of the*
# MYSTIC

*Reconnecting to the Spirit of Life and
Walking Your Sacred Path*

# the book of nature

If you read just one book in this
life, let it be the book of nature.
The secrets of the entire Universe
are waiting for you there.

In spring, summer, fall, and winter.
In birth, in death, in sunrise and sunset.
In the plants, the trees,
the animals, and the flowers.
In the waters, the fire,
the wind, and the stars.

And because you are nature,
they are waiting within you too.

△

# THE RETURN OF THE MYSTIC

*'The eye through which I see God is the same eye*
*through which God sees me; my eye and God's eye*
*are one eye, one seeing, one knowing, one love.'*

MEISTER ECKHART

Throughout my life I've had unexplainable mystical experiences in which it felt as if the sacred was teaching me directly and guiding me through my intuition. And it was while I was in nature that I felt this connection with the sacred most strongly. If I felt disconnected from my heart and soul or if there was something on which I wanted to receive guidance, I'd go into nature to find the answer I was seeking.

In the past, although I was fascinated by God, whenever I tried to walk a path that positioned the divine as above me or separate from me, as some external being I needed to bow to, the gates wouldn't open. Now, three decades on from my first spiritual awakening as a teen, I see that my journey has always been guiding me to see the sacred that's already here, all around us – in the plants, the trees, the flowers, the water, the sun, the stars, and the sky.

I've always been drawn to nature as a gateway to connect with what I now call the unseen world. From a young age, I'd directly channel what I received from nature through my creations. When I was in my early twenties and living in Sydney, Australia, I'd sit by the ocean and as the waves rolled in and out, I'd subtly receive an answer to the question that was most pressing on my mind. And years later, in the exquisite parks of London, as I admired the beautiful spring flowers as they burst from their buds, I'd receive inspiration, encouragement, and fully formed creative ideas that would have taken me hours of thinking time sat at my desk.

However, I wasn't taught this practice of connecting with nature to connect with my inner wisdom – I did it naturally, almost as if I remembered it, and that's because it comes from an innate place. I strongly believe that every single one of us has the natural ability to connect with the Unseen Spirit of Nature to receive guidance, support, and connection. And that we can all tap into the unseen world if we just open our hearts and minds.

This is the path of the mystic – to go direct to the sacred to embody the unseen. I believe we've all experienced connecting with this unseen spiritual world of nature and that, on more occasions than we could possibly recall, we've had a sense of oneness with Life through being in nature.

Society tells us to look outside of ourselves for guidance and answers, and we're bombarded with external messages and noise daily. We've become so disconnected from the wise, intelligent pulse of the Earth, the natural world, and the sacred Earth-based wisdom teachings of our ancestry, that we've forgotten how to do this incredibly natural thing. As a result, most of us have learned not to see the sacred pulse of Life that's all around us, below us, above us and within us.

Humanity is at an interesting stage in which it seems like every religion or spiritual lineage has a guru who's fallen from grace, and where all spiritual paths have been tainted by some kind of wrongdoing. This often happens when we put people on a godly pedestal. I wonder if we're rightly tearing down the structures and systems that stop us from seeing the sacred as something that's innate and available for us all to connect with. The divine has long been positioned as something outside us and special rather than within and natural. But the sacred is within all living things, within nature, and within you too. And if we turn our gaze below, around, and within, and honor the sacred as Life itself, it will change so much for us individually, collectively, and as a planet.

*We're all being called to open our senses, our hearts, and our minds to the secrets of the cosmos and to the magic that can be found in nature if we open our hearts to see it. Both physically and spiritually.*

To see the sacred that's already here and connect with the wisdom that's always been waiting for us within. And to reconnect with nature as our teacher and our guide. Once you do this, you'll see that you are never alone on this interconnected planet spinning in the ordered Universe with such unfathomable precision, mystery, and grace.

I'm a mystic. My path is and always has been one of direct experience of the sacred and being led by the wisdom within. There have been many times when I wished it was more linear and less physical; like most of us, I've longed for an instruction manual. But it seems that my soul's path is to go direct to the sacred and to remind others that they can do this too.

I believe that we're intuitive, mystical beings, and that we come in that way. And that most of us, at some stage, get separated from this true nature and stop living in accordance with the sacred intelligence of our soul. I believe that our soul chose to be here, in this body, on this planet, at this time, in this ancestry, and that our purpose is to stay connected to our soul and invite it to incarnate more fully while we're here.

I believe that the best book you'll ever read is the book of nature. It's waiting for you to explore in every petal, leaf, and river. I believe that all the secrets of the Universe can be found in the mystery school of nature. May we wake up to this before it's too late.

Just as the caterpillar has imaginal cells that know how to transform, I believe that all of nature has these too. There's a lot of talk about creating a new Earth; however, I don't think it's our planet that needs to be reborn, it's humanity. And the 'New Earth' is actually more ancient than we are. Maybe you're a part of the team of souls who came here to awaken humanity to this transformation and shift in consciousness.

As we trust the imaginal cells of our own transformation to rebirth ourselves anew, to wake up from our slumber, may we all play our part in weaving the sacred threads of heaven and Earth back together. May the Sacred Feminine and Sacred Masculine come into balance. May we return to the arms of the Goddess. May our mystical hearts awaken wider and wider with each new day. May we stop resisting change and slow down to the pace of the Earth so we can remember that before we came here, our soul had a dream and our life, this life, is it.

# △
# AWAKENING YOUR MYSTICAL HEART

This life is but a breath in the spiritual journey of the soul. Somehow, your soul managed to be here, in this body, on this planet, at this time. And what a time you chose to come. The path of the mystic is the path of the heart. An open heart lets more love in and with that comes heartbreak too.

The mystic is dedicated to letting Life soften them and open them. For the mystic longs to experience the highs and the lows, summer and winter, spring and fall; it's as if they remember that they came here to truly live it *all*, to feel it all, to witness it all, to love it all. Through all the extremes.

Led by the intelligence of winter, fall, and the dark nights, the mystic surrenders who they thought they were so that they can truly live. Reborn again and again, they become more childlike the older they get, for they endeavor to see this planet with the awe and wonder of a child, which means they connect with the Spirit of Life rather than letting life harden their hearts. You can see by the light in someone's eyes how connected they are with the Spirit of Life.

Our society's obsession with the cult of youth is so messed up – in clinging on to the physical we cut ourselves off from the mystical Spirit of Life. And the mystical is where the real youth is. Where the real life-force is. And this has nothing to do with time or age. For the mystic connects with nature and nature is constantly being born anew. Nature doesn't resist the decay of fall and the death of winter. It resurrects itself every year, and we can do that too. Perhaps it's our fixation on youth and spring and summer that's stopping us from truly living.

When the mystic experiences heartbreak or sorrow, they do their best not to bypass it or let it harden them. They do their best not to close off their heart to the world or separate. They endeavor to find ways to welcome and widen. Mystics see Life itself as the teacher and their experience of it as the syllabus and take notes along the way. They know that the heart is intelligent and connected to the sacred pulse of Life. And that if we close off our hearts to avoid pain, we also close ourselves off from Life. We disconnect and separate, little by little, from the Spirit of Life and our life-force decreases.

*Mystics are open to exploring life's biggest questions and letting life reveal its wisdom to them. They know that the sacred isn't out of reach but something they can experience in themselves directly.*

Mystics exist within all faith paths and outside of them too. They're hungry to become intimate with the divine, to merge with it, to embody it, and to let it guide their life. The American Franciscan friar and author Father Richard Rohr says that the word mystic means one who has moved from mere belief systems or belonging systems to actual inner experience. This is the way of the mystic – to go within, to be led by the intuitive, potent, intelligent, mystical heart. To commune directly with the Spirit of Life.

The mystic may read books, but ultimately, they're sacred adventurers who are more interested in cultivating insight than merely gaining linear intellect. Mystics aren't just open to learning new things, they're also open to 'unlearning' and loosening their grip on what they thought they knew for sure.

The mystic knows that they're not separate from Life and that the Spirit of Life is always available to guide them. The mystic is led from the wisdom that's forever whispering within, and while they may choose to worship at a particular physical temple, they don't need that to connect with the sacred, for the sacred is everywhere and within everything. The path of the mystic is to live with an open heart and mind. To be curious and surprised. The mystic seeks states of awe and wonder and sees each new day and each new thing as a fascinating mystery rather than a certainty. It's as if they remember that they're here for the great adventure of life on Earth and are exploring and experiencing every step of the way.

The mystic isn't set in their ways; they revolt against rigidity and systems that don't allow their heart to stay open and their true nature to be expressed. They haven't forgotten how to play, question, and create. And while creativity may be part of their vocation, the type of creativity that brings them the most joy is one without an attachment to the outcome.

Mystics exist within all parts of society, and some are the courageous ones who challenge the status quo. They're the rule breakers, the rebels, the wise ones, and the menders. Light bearers of humanity, they're the artists, the singers, the poets, the dancers. They're the dreamers, the lovers, the system disruptors, the cycle breakers, the activists. They're the visionaries, the healers, the seers, and the nature lovers.

## SOUL INQUIRY

*What does your mystical heart want you to know today?*

When she kissed the Earth
her head dropped lower than her heart
and she connected to the temple within.

*the inner temple* △

# △
# YOU CAN GO DIRECT

*'You don't worship the gate. You go into the inner temple.'*

RAM DASS

The mystic longs to have a direct experience of the sacred, and they know that they can do that in any moment of any day, simply by gazing at a flower or sitting with a tree. The mystic sees this life as a mystery school for the soul. And while they may discover teachers and books to guide them along their journey, they know that they don't need these to reach the sacred, for in any chosen moment they can go direct.

In the timeline of the soul, this life is but a moment, and the awakening process never ends; it's a journey, not a destination for souls to reach. So often on our awakening path we strive to arrive at a place. To attain some new level or more enlightened state. As if there's something we need to know or figure out, learn or remember; a frequency that we'll arrive at if we do enough of a particular practice or sit at the feet of the right teacher, or rely on an external spiritual tool to reveal our destiny to us. It's as if our natural state of being is not enough, or not sacred.

But what if there's no place at which to arrive? What if the sacred has always been waiting for us here? Above us, below us, around us, and within us. What if God is actually the Unseen Spirit of Life?

**What if we realized that this whole time, there are no gates to the temple, for it's always been within?**

What if the sacred is also encoded in our bodies? From our bones to our mitochondria (the powerhouses of our cells); from the unique harmonics of our voice to the presence of our soul, which could be felt the moment our soul arrived Earth-side; and from the freckles on our face to the kink in our hair. Perhaps this is the point of the darkest nights: to dim it all down so that we've no choice but to dig deep and find the sacred in all living things. On Earth as it is in heaven.

*You came in sacred, and you still are sacred.*
*Everything is, for it has within it the Spirit of Life.*
*Somewhere along the way humanity forgot this.*

We stopped seeing the sacred in ourselves, in each other, in nature, and all around us. For many of us, when we arrived Earth-side, the people who welcomed us had forgotten how to witness it, for those who had greeted *them* had been welcomed by ones who had forgotten too. But the sacred was in you then and it's in you now too.

## THE SEVERING

This age in which we're living is an interesting one. So much harm has been done to the Earth-based Indigenous wisdom teachings of numerous cultures, and as a result, we've forgotten to see the sacred in the rivers and the trees, in the flowers and the bees, in the coming and going of the seasons, in the rising and setting of the sun, in the exhale and inhale of our breath from birth until death.

So many of us can feel the ache caused by our severing from the Earth-based wisdom teachings of our ancient ancestors, who lived in deep reverence to the sacred above and below, around and within; who sat together in circle around a fire; who were humbled by the wondrous expanse of the starlit night sky. To them, the gateways of birth and death were sacred, for the Spirit of Life was revered and intact.

*I believe that there's an unconscious grief, a pain, a deep longing, to be held by something – something sacred – while we're here on Earth.*

We might externalize this ache by clinging on to relationships or substances outside of ourselves, but I sense that it runs deep within most of us. It comes not only from the separation we feel from each other but also from the sacred Spirit of Life itself.

For too long the sacred has been hidden and the Divine Feminine banished underground, and in this time, we've caused so much harm to this planet. And now I believe that many of our hearts are breaking and awakening to see it. Perhaps including yours. But if enough of us see it, if enough of us devote ourselves to honoring it, perhaps this universal organism of which we're all a part will reorganize and remember and re-experience itself for what it is: a sacred miracle experiencing itself in the physical.

There's been so much persecution in the name of the sacred that staying connected with it and seeing it as normal has become near impossible. Or painful. Or risky. So much fear, shame, confusion, misunderstanding, and mistruth are cloaked around the sacred that it's hard to find our way back to it. But we will. Your being here with me, reading this, is evidence that it's happening.

One by one we're seeking a direct experience of the sacred and understanding that it's our right to go direct. One by one, we're returning to the mystery school of nature and choosing to see the sacred that's already here. On Earth as it is in heaven. Can you hear your ancient ancestors singing you on?

And while it's important to acknowledge the severing from the Earth and the harm that's been caused, particularly in the name of the sacred, it's also crucial that we find our way back to it in an intimate and lasting way. When you develop a direct relationship with the sacred, no one can take it away from you – it's a connection so innate that you'll have it for life.

When I was in my early twenties, I started noticing the documentaries that were being made about the state of the planet and the assertion that collectively, we seemed to be waking up. And I'll never forget the powerful, familiar voice I heard, saying, 'It's happening. This is why we came here, at this time. There's still time for us to turn this around – to awaken and create this much-needed shift.' Maybe you're one of the torchbearers here to awaken and activate this much-needed shift. Your presence and action can do it. Tend your connection with the Spirit of Life within and be led.

## SOUL INQUIRY

*What, if anything, were you told about God/Goddess/*
*Spirit/the sacred while you were growing up?*

*What do you believe now?*

# you were never kicked
# out of the garden

What if we realized that the trees speak sacred?
That the flowers speak sacred.
That the waters speak sacred.
That the animals speak sacred.
That the stars speak sacred.
That all of nature and all of Life speak sacred.
And because you're part of Life,
you speak sacred too.

## △
# SEEING THE SACRED
# THAT'S ALREADY HERE

Western civilization has indoctrinated us to regard 'the exotic' as superior and what's hard to find as valuable, but if we look closely at our immediate surroundings, we may discover that what we're seeking, what we're hungry for, has been waiting for us there all along. We just need to open our eyes to see the sacred that's already here.

When I began my herbalism training, my mind was blown open as I observed my own relationship with nature, the land, and the plants I consumed. One of the herbs I worked with frequently was nettle, which is a powerful, nourishing plant. At first, I ordered nettle leaf online and had no idea where the plant came from or what it looked like. Next, I found a local herbal shop, Starchild, and a month or so later, I began seeing nettles growing in a lane on my morning walk.

I'll never forget the morning I opened my front door and saw nettles growing through the crack in a paving stone! It was an extremely humbling moment as I realized that nature was already providing but I didn't have the eyes to see it.

I had the same experience when I was diagnosed with pelvic prolapse following my daughter's birth. I pulled together a healing regimen that included drinking and bathing in herbal infusions made with a plant commonly known as lady's mantle, which I hadn't worked with before. I bought some lady's mantle from Starchild and began drinking my infusions daily, and I also looked at pictures of the plant and connected with its spirit as I drank it.

Then one day as I was walking around our garden with my son, I saw a new plant beginning to grow and I recognized the tiny leaf of lady's mantle. I cried out with joy that nature had offered the very plant my body most revered and needed! Perhaps that plant had always been there, but once more, I didn't have the eyes to see it. Or maybe when I connected with the spirit of the plant and thus to the Spirit of Life, nature did what it does best and provided!

We all have Earth-based wisdom teachings in our ancestry, most of which have been stolen, silenced, or severed through colonialism, patriarchy, and time. I've always felt an ache for those in my lineage and I believe this is what led me to travel to the lands of my ancestors at a young age. However, it wasn't until I started studying herbalism and working with the plants beneath my feet that I experienced a real remembering and unlocking of this lineage lost and a deepening into proper ancestral healing.

It was as if through working with the same plants that my ancient ancestors had, I could reach back to them and mend within my cells what had been severed. It felt as though with every tea meditation, every occasion I wrote with the flowers and the trees, each time I prayed with the water or placed my hands on the stones, I could hear their whispers more and more. Every time I learned to identify and harvest a plant, every time I bent down to forage and do the repetitive movements that my ancient ancestors had done, it opened the field of connection with the lost wisdom of my lineage. The wisdom that was forbidden to be passed down.

## SOUL INQUIRY

*Nature and the Spirit of Life are always available to open to us and through us. Look around you right now. Can you see the sacred that's already here – below you, around you, and within you?*

*What message does it have for you?*

Do all the churches and temples,
gurus, and godheads need to fall
for us to remember that this whole time,
the sacred has always been
within all living things?

*becoming golden* △

# △
# COMPARTMENTALIZATION
# OF SPIRIT AND MATTER

I hope the day will come when words like mystic, sacred, and the divine become obsolete. No longer needed because the sacred, the unseen, the mystical is felt and known intrinsically. When heaven and Earth are woven back together. When the sacred is seen as a normal part of life. Both extraordinary and ordinary at the same time.

For the sacred is within all things, all moments, all beings. The sacred is in every breath, every birth, every sunrise and sunset. The sacred is in every flower that opens, every tree that grows, every river that flows, in every night and every day, in every I love you, and in every heartbreak, too.

When I was young, I yearned for something without being able to put words around it. As a child I'd sometimes tell my mum that I'd come here for a reason, but I couldn't remember exactly why or how I knew. Like so many of us, perhaps including you, I felt a deep, ancient soul yearning, burrowed in the chambers of my heart and the marrow of my bones, for a way of living that I innately knew but had not yet found. I'm not sure if it was something I came in remembering or something that was calling me forth.

It took four decades of living and searching for me to discover that what I was yearning for was to exist in a world where the sacred is a normal part of life. Where we realize that we didn't get kicked out of the garden and that the sacred was and is already here.

The word 'theanthropic', derived from Greek words meaning god-man, describes the state of being fully human and fully divine at the same time.

Two equally significant parts. Not separate. Together. Whole. One. And when I reflect on my spiritual journey, I can see that while the awakening processes I experienced invited new capacities to open and my consciousness to expand, the sacred and the physical remained compartmentalized. Mind, body, and soul were not one. The sacred was unwoven from my everyday life.

Now, like you, I'm living in a time when we're largely starved of the sacred. It's been unwoven from our culture and society, and I believe this is one of the problems with the world right now. And it's why the simple act of seeing the sacred that's already here – above us, below us, around us, within us – is a revolutionary act. I believe that endeavoring to tend the Spirit of Life and the spirit within others has the power to change the world.

## REWEAVING THE SACRED THREAD

When I had my first awakening as a teenager, it felt like a whole new world had opened up, which was incredible. But it was as if I became disconnected from the world I was currently in, too. And when I look back on my early years as a channel and healer, when I was committed to living in alignment with my soul, following my intuition and truly living a spiritual life, I can see how disjointed they were. However, it wasn't until I began consciously working with plants through studying herbalism, and became a mother, that I saw just how much.

During the early months of the COVID-19 pandemic, I was on one of my daily walks in nature below the belly of Glastonbury Tor (the sacred hill above the town), when the realization literally stopped me in my tracks as I crossed a field strewn with buttercups. As a sleep-deprived new mum, I was feeling so torn between that new role and my soul mission/career. Until that point, I'd chosen a life of service and deep contemplation. My daily spiritual practice was non-negotiable, and it had nourished and served me so well; however, now I was unable to show up to it for as long and in the same way as I did before I had a child.

Walking among the wildflowers with Sunny wrapped to my chest, I saw how even after so many years on a spiritual path, there was still a separation between my spiritual practice and my everyday life. I also saw how for so many of us our spiritual practices are devoid of nature as a gateway to the sacred, and rather than working with what's around us, our ceremonies are so particular: we feel that to get them 'right' we must buy the thing from the shop or order it from some faraway land. In that field on that day, I saw how disconnected from the sacred Spirit of Life we've become.

Then I kept hearing a phrase: 'Weave the sacred all the way back in. Weave the sacred into everyday life.' I took this to mean find ways to see the sacred that's already here. To see the sacred in every moment rather than trying to escape reality by going off to 'be spiritual' or 'do something spiritual.' To see all that happens in the messiness of our lives as an opportunity to return to the sacred.

> **By connecting with nature (all living things) we can weave the sacred into our everyday lives and see it as both ordinary and extraordinary.**

The difference was subtle yet huge, hard to describe but deeply felt. Over the next year I made it my mission to reweave the sacred into all parts of my life. My challenge was to see the sacred in every single moment – on my walks as I passed the flowers and plants and when I I gazed into my son's eyes at bath time. I created altars using items in my kitchen cupboard and things fallen in my garden. I found ways to engage more deeply with people in my life whom I'd previously labeled as 'not spiritual' and therefore uninterested in going deep.

I decompartmentalized the physical from the spiritual, the mundane from the magical, Earth from heaven, body from spirit, mother from mystic. I saw how so much of my life and this world had been severed, separated, and boxed in. How the programming of this planet and the time we came into has resulted in us labeling, comparing, and disconnecting. And how it's possible for us to mend if we find ways to weave the sacred thread all the way in.

About six months after my realization, I was mentoring my friend Annabelle Shaman, a proud Aboriginal woman, as she was writing her book *The Future Ancestor.* Our publisher had instructed her to be as 'mystical' as she wished, but Annabelle had not heard the word mystical before and asked me what it meant. I explained that from my perspective she was simply being encouraged to trust her channel and to be as poetic as she wanted to.

Don't try to follow a specific way of writing, I advised her, just trust the whispers of your ancestors and be led. Annabelle also asked one of her elders this question and I was deeply moved when they told her that mystical is a word that white people use to describe the most normal thing in the world: Yuma, or oneness with Mother Earth.

Spirit of Life, mother of us all, sacred pulse, God, life-force, divine. May our children's children grow up in a world where the Unseen Spirit of Life isn't regarded as something special to reach for or one day attain but instead is so deeply woven into everyday life that they realize that they, and all of Life, *are* it. May they see it in all living things. In the plants, the trees, the stones, and the flowers. In the waters and the wind. In the mountains and the ocean. In all animals and all people. If we can somehow manage to see the sacred that is, was, and always will be right here on Earth, then maybe the future for humanity will be golden and bright.

## SOUL INQUIRY

*What's one simple way that you can weave the sacred more fully into your everyday life?*

*How compartmentalized is your spiritual life from the rest of your life?*

What if there was no creator?
What if God was actually in all of nature?

You are nature.
Every living thing is nature.
The entire cosmos is nature.

What if God is actually the
Unseen Spirit of Life?

*hidden in plain sight* △

# △
# THE UNSEEN SPIRIT OF LIFE

There's an intelligent, sacred pulse woven through all of Life. It tells the flowers to open and close, the seasons to come and go, and the planet to spin. It guides the coming and going of the tides, the waxing and waning of the moon, and the dance of the constellations. This sacred intelligence tells the trees how to reach their roots deep and their branches high. It tells babies how to take their first breath and their bodies how to grow.

This sacred, intelligent pulse is within all living things – it's life-force itself and one of the greatest mysteries there is. It was present when you took your first breath, and it will be there as you exhale your last. This intelligent pulse of Life has captivated humanity since the beginning. It is itself ineffable and yet, if we open our eyes and hearts, it's impossible to ignore. In fact, attempting to name, claim, and put a label on this indescribable force has caused great harm through the ages.

When we're connected to that, we're connected to Life itself. When we're connected to that, we're connected to our intuition. When we're connected to that, we're connected to our sacred purpose. When we're connected to that, we're living a mystical life. When we're connected to that, we're weaving the sacred more fully in.

When we become disconnected from this intelligence, we become disconnected from life-force itself, and we feel isolated, alone, stuck, and separate – from ourselves, each other, and the planet. It feels as though something's missing. And that something is our connection with the Spirit of Life. With the sacred essence that's present in all living things. From star to river, planet to seed, nature is Life itself. This planet is part of the knowable and unknowable Universe and so are we. And so are all things in nature.

*If we're disconnected from the nature around us on Earth, then we're also disconnected from the nature of the cosmos, for all is part of a greater whole.*

I wonder if the separation we feel from one another and indeed from ourselves can be soothed by seeing ourselves as part of it all. By seeing our planet as a tiny part of something so vast and miraculous that we cannot possibly fathom its immensity. A mere cell in the cosmic organism called Life.

Many mystical writings speak of the insanity of relying on our own strength or will over the order of the cosmos. This idea/truth brings me a lot of relief when I'm anxious or if I'm trying to control things, especially when it feels like life's falling apart. In all these moments we have a choice either to rely on our own will or strength by trying to control things or surrender to the mysterious intelligence that causes the Earth to spin and our fingernails to grow.

Perhaps when humans were separated from the garden of the Earth, perhaps when we saw nature as something separate from us, perhaps when we stopped living in reverence to the cycles of nature, we became disconnected from the Spirit of Life around us and within us. The Spirit of Life, this ancient pulse that's always existed and will never not, it's always calling us back to it. Do you hear it? It's never stopped beating from within. Listen with your inner ear. See with your inner heart. Place your palm on a tree, open your heart to a flower, turn your gaze to the rising sun. Simple acts like this resync you to it. Align your life to that sacred beat. Take your pulse from that. Keep choosing to reconnect with that. Choose to return, again and again, back to yourself and all of Life, through the sacred law of nature.

It's time to remember how to recognize the sacred that's always been here and return to the wisdom that's always been waiting within. To wake up to the realization that perhaps this life is something our soul dreamed of, and, no matter where we are, we can find a way to discover that there's something sacred here.

## SOUL INQUIRY

*What in your life increases your life-force?*

*What in your life diminishes your life-force?*

*When do you most feel connected to the sacred within?*

△

# WE ARE NATURE

We've built a world on top of the world. If you look up the word nature in a dictionary, you'll find that one definition is 'all the plants, animals, and physical features on the Earth, as well as its forces and processes.' You'll also see that this definition doesn't just omit humans, it specifically states that we're not part of nature. That we're separate from it. We speak of 'getting into nature' or 'getting grounded' as things we need to do. We've forgotten that we don't exist *in* nature, we *are* nature.

Is it any wonder that humanity has caused so much harm to this planet when we regard ourselves as an extension of it? Is it surprising that so many of us feel disconnected and alone when we see the sacred as an external single male God in the sky rather than something that's woven into every living thing; as a place to ascend to rather than innately within; as something we can reach only when we die rather than one that's available to us every moment of every day?

I believe that this is the real separation that so many of us feel – from the Earth itself, from the Great Mother and perhaps the archetype of Mother, from the wisdom teachings of our ancestry, from our elders and ancestors, and from ourselves and each other. I think that it's our seeing humanity as separate from the Earth and her cyclic ways that's caused many of the problems that we face today. And that the way we treat the Earth, the feminine, great cycles such as the seasons, and initiatory gateways such as pregnancy, birth, aging, grief, and death is directly related to this.

Are we finally waking up to the harm that our emphasis on spring and summer over fall and winter, on producing over creating, on machines over mystics, on certainty over mystery, and on taking over giving is inflicting on humanity and the planet? I believe that now more than ever we need to notice the breathtaking beauty that's all around us. To weave the sacred back into our everyday lives.

Reach back to the ones in your ancestry who were connected to the spirit of all living things. The wise ones who tended the land and lived in reverence to the sacred woven through it all. Despite the tragic harm caused by colonialism and patriarchy, there are still Indigenous wisdom keepers (living and past) who hold this thread. May we protect, support, and revere them. May we listen deeply to their song.

## EARTH-BASED WISDOM

In its simplest form, animism (the belief that all beings in the Universe, including humans, animals, plants, land, and water, possess a spirit) speaks to the soul. It whispers a sacred truth that every part of the natural world, from the grandest mountains to the humblest river stones, is alive with a spiritual essence. The word animism comes from the Latin word 'anima,' meaning 'breath' or 'spirit,' and conceptually, animism paints a vibrant picture of a world in which everything and everyone is connected.

Animism is practiced, in different forms, in most of the world's Indigenous traditions, and it teaches us that communication with the spirit world isn't only possible but essential. Animist cultures maintain a deep-seated respect for ancestors, believing that even after death, their forebears continue to exist in spirit form; the ancestors' wisdom and guidance are available to us, if only we remember to listen.

Animism was once sidelined by Western thinkers as a 'primitive' form of spirituality (a view that one could argue has caused more devastation, destruction, and separation to humanity and this planet than anything else), but we're finally beginning to appreciate its profound respect for the environment and the insights it offers on the interconnectedness of Life.

The ancient philosophical concept of *anima mundi* speaks of the existence of a 'world soul' and an innate connection between all living beings; it holds that since every individual human has a soul, so too must the world itself. This way of seeing things acknowledges that everything, not only humans, possesses a soul, consciousness, spirit, or sacred essence. The plants that breathe life into our air, the animals that share our environment, and the so-called 'inanimate' things too – the mountains, waters, stones, and more – they all carry an intelligent, sacred spark that calls for our respect and reverence.

> *Nature is alive and available for us to be in communion with it. If we see the sacred essence in the life around us, that same essence becomes more alive within us too.*

This is why we feel more ourselves after spending time in nature and why we're able to tap into our intuition more clearly when we do. Many of our ancestors, rooted in cultures across the world – from the mountains of Siberia to the lochs of Scotland, from the plains of North America to the deserts of Africa, from the stone circles of Britain to the sacred wells of France, from the red earth of Australia to the hidden valleys of Asia – understood this. They built their lives on the foundations of animism, recognizing that each living being, each element of nature, carried its own unique spirit.

Our ancestors' way of living was a testament to the profound inter-connectedness of all Life. And I believe that the plants, trees, flowers, waters, stars, and stones carry this lost wisdom, and that through working with nature, we can return to our own true nature and unlock the secret of the Universe, for they exist within our soul and our cells.

I believe that by reconnecting with nature we're reconnecting with the sacred intelligence that was present when we drew our first breath and was also present at the birth of the Earth. I believe that through reconnecting with nature we can reach back to our positive ancestors, the ones who didn't forget, and receive wisdom and holding from them too. Remember that you are nature and that you'll always find your true nature in nature.

Tragically, many Earth-based wisdom lineages and cultures have been lost. In my own Scottish, Irish, and Nordic ancestry, worship of nature as living Goddess was forbidden, and reverence of the Sacred Feminine became dormant due to silencing. Healers, shamans, witches, herbalists, medicine people, midwives, and those who worked with plants to heal and lived in harmony with the Earth were persecuted and their cultural practices forbidden or wiped out.

This is the history we inherited. Perhaps it's our resistance to the natural world and the changing nature within us that causes this severing, and this is the deepest ache we feel. And while consciousness is always changing and we can change only what we're conscious of, we're only just beginning to understand the extreme damage that's been done.

Recently, the First Minister of Scotland made a public apology to the descendants of the Scottish people who had been persecuted as witches during the Middle Ages, some of whom were my paternal ancestors. Wise women and men who were killed for practicing their traditions and seeing the sacred in the Earth.

## THE WEB OF LIFE

When I reflect on the emergency that the Earth faces today because of pollution, fracking, climate change, ecocide, and so much more, it makes me wonder if the reason we as a species have caused such harm to this planet is because of the severing of the Sacred Feminine and the Earth. Is it the disempowerment of women as Goddess that's left us hungry for the fullness of our mothers and our sacred connection with Mother Earth? If we truly saw everything as sacred, would we be in this situation globally? And if, during the colonial era, Indigenous peoples had not been regarded as lesser beings but as wisdom keepers in sacred union with the Spirit of Life, would this planet be different today?

If you study the great mystics, philosophers, poets, inventors, scientists, and sages through the ages, you'll recognize a common theme echoing back: flower, tree, water, star, moon, fire, stone – nature was a source of inspiration, communion, and connection for them all. Many shared how the wisdom of the Universe could be touched by gazing at the night sky or communing with a tree.

In my personal journey as a mystic, the deeper I spiral inward, the more humbled I am by the vast wisdom that's available to us if we turn our gaze down to the Earth and within. If we remember that the cells that make up the four chambers of the heart consist of ancient exploding stars. If we use the land and our hearts as a guide and a compass. If we connect with the intelligent, sacred pulse that's never stopped beating within it all.

*Nature reminds us of the enormity and interconnectedness of the Earth and all Life, which can shift our perspective and diminish feelings of isolation or overwhelm.*

Our connection with the larger web of Life can bring comfort, solace, and perspective, reducing anxiety and promoting a broader sense of well-being. I believe that no matter who you are, you can develop a direct relationship with the Spirit of Life. No matter who you are, in nature you'll likely hear your intuition more clearly. No matter who you are, in seeing the sacred that's all around you, you'll discover your sacred purpose without even trying.

We're being called back to the Earth and the arms of the Goddess to weave the sacred back in, to weave nature back into the center of our everyday lives.

To see ourselves as nature, and to spend more time interacting with the living natural world – returning to nature.

How's your connection with nature? What's your relationship with your own body? Can you live in a more grounded way? How can you actively spend time in the natural world around you, tend it, and take your place as one of its custodians? How can you see the sacred in all of Life, notice the changing seasons around you and within you, remember that you too are part of the Earth's ever-changing landscape? How can you embrace your body as your home and the planet as your Mother?

## SOUL INQUIRY

*Growing up, what were you taught about nature?*

*What do you believe about nature now?*

*What's your earliest or fondest childhood memory about nature?*

# nature was her church

Trees were her cathedrals.
The long grass, her rosary.
Flowers, her prayer book.
The sky, her domed ceiling.
The birds, her choir.
The stone circle, her confessional.
The river, where she baptized herself.

She knew that God was in nature.
That everything was nature.
And that the temple was always
waiting for her within.

# △
# THE UNSEEN SPIRIT OF NATURE

There's more to nature than what can be seen with our eyes. If you watch carefully when the sun rises, you'll find it difficult not to sense it. There's the beauty of the seen world of nature but beyond the veil is a whole other world – the unseen world of nature, the unseen *nature* of nature. And you can connect with it every moment of every day.

The seen and unseen worlds are intertwined – they cannot be torn apart. As the ancient hermetic law of correspondence says, 'As above, so below; as below, so above.' If the seen is there, so too is the unseen. And the same applies to us. When the body is alive, so is the soul. And when nature is present, so is the Spirit of Life. Have you ever wondered why we're so captivated by the flickering flames of a fire or in awe of the first tree blossom each spring? Could it be that the Spirit of Life is present in these moments too?

*I believe that the Unseen Spirit of Nature can guide you to return to your true nature, reconnect with the sacred pulse of Life, reconnect with your intuition, and live your most authentic life.*

Pay attention to the parts of nature that you're most drawn to work with, and also those that surprise you the most! And always trust your intuition and your own timing when it comes to what you work with and when. I believe that intuition is connected to our soul, to our innate intelligence, and that this part of us chose to be here and is available to guide us every moment of every day. And that when we're in nature it's easier to connect with our intuition.

There are two reasons why this happens: *presence* and *purpose*. When we're in nature it's easier to be present because nature is always in the present moment. Flowers don't try to stay tight in their buds and trees don't try to hold on to their leaves; they're always in the present moment. Change is their natural state. And it's in the present moment that our intuition is waiting for us. The mind is all about the future and the past, but if we're able to drop fully into the present moment, in most cases, our intuition will rise gently within without us even trying.

Nature is so pure in its ability to 'be,' that by connecting with nature we're able to connect with the Spirit of Life that's available to guide us every moment of every day. We can reconnect with our own life-force and true nature. And because we're all unique, the more we can embrace our true nature, the more we'll embrace our unique path, which is where we'll find our purpose.

## SOUL INQUIRY

*How can you acknowledge the Unseen Spirit of Nature around, below, above, and within you a little bit more right now?*

# △
# LIVING THE QUESTIONS

A mystic is dedicated to entering communion and union with the sacred. Embodied spirit. They're devoted to merging with the Spirit of Life and partaking in a direct dance with Life itself. They live with an open mind and heart. They're willing to ask the big questions, but they don't wait to receive finite answers to them. Instead, they embrace the great mystery and exploration and choose to truly live into their questions experientially.

The phrase 'live the questions' comes from one of my favorite books, *Letters to a Young Poet* by Rainer Maria Rilke. In one of the poems in the book, Rilke invites the reader not to seek the answers to life's big questions but instead to 'live the questions' and allow the answers to emerge over time.

To live the questions means to fully engage with the uncertainties of life rather than simply seeking quick or easy answers. It invites us to be open to experience, to explore and reflect, and to acknowledge that the journey itself can be just as valuable as any destination. In essence, it encourages a state of curiosity, wonder, and humility as we navigate the complexities of being human.

Living the questions is what mystics have done through the ages and in my opinion it's how some of the most brilliant minds and wise ones have stumbled across their findings, inventions, and creations. Anyone who has been on the spiritual journey for a while knows that it never ends and that the more we learn, the more the questions emerge.

*Living the questions is a way of life and it's one of the foundations of being an embodied mystic or someone who's truly living a soul-led life.*

All the intuition and insights in the world are pointless without integration, embodiment, and grounded action. When we LIVE the questions, we stop waiting for the answers and instead choose to live INTO them. We take baby steps and let life reveal itself to us through the living. We enter a co-creative dance with Life. We merge with the sacred rather than separating ourselves off from it. We enter a world of wonder and awe instead of expecting certainty every moment of every day.

When we live the questions, instead of praying for guidance from an external source or looking to those wiser or more experienced than us for a finite answer, we enter deep communion with the Spirit of Life. We enter a state of wonder. We open ourselves up to living the questions and letting life deliver the answers to us and through us rather than remaining rigid and expecting to have the journey perfectly mapped out before we take the next step.

To live the questions is to live a mystical life. To live a mystical life is to enter communion with the Spirit of Life. You know that you're not separate from this great intelligence and that you'll always be led. This is how we walk our sacred path.

## SOUL INQUIRY

*Which question are you living into now?*

# △
# SEEING THE SACRED IN OTHERS

While we can't possibly know for sure, I believe that our souls have experienced and known places different from just here now. I believe that the soul chose to be here and that it longs to be recognized and seen. For through witnessing comes connection, and Life is connected.

During the first 18 months of his life, my son and I shared a nightly bath. I'd glide him through the silky water as a way of easing his transition from the watery world of my womb to the land and air world that he was adjusting to. One night I began to sing a song that became *his* song. The melody was simple, and the lyrics went like this: 'Thank you for visiting me on Earth, baby.' Each time I sang it, Sunny would become weightless, melt into my arms, and the most contented look would appear on his face.

I'm sure that moments like this are the ones that will come to me in my last breaths. I often found myself crying at the sweetness of this in-between time and how in witnessing him I too was being witnessed.

In our modern world, the soul is starved of being truly seen and we're starved of the soul. This disconnection can make us feel more separate, severed, and hungry for connection. This hunger leads us to reach for things outside of ourselves to satiate us. This hurt and disconnection are the things that lead us to cause so much harm to each other and the planet. If only we knew how to truly connect.

The quickest way back to the sacred is to notice it in those around us. To seek the Spirit of Life everywhere. In the people we meet, in the animals we encounter, in the trees, the stones, the waters, and the flowers. Be someone who witnesses the spirit, the sacred, the soul, the consciousness in all living things. When you do this, you'll likely find that life becomes more amazing and alive, and you do too. Seek the Spirit of Life and it will seek you.

## SOUL INQUIRY

*Who in your life truly sees you?*

*How can you do the same for someone else today?*

# peace on earth begins at birth

What if when we arrived Earth-side,
our soul was recognized?

Welcomed by ones who were remembered.
Cradled by beings who didn't need to awaken
because they never fell asleep.

What if the hands that touched us
knew they were touching the
Universe ordered as the cosmos?

Made of cell and star, soil and soul.
A bridge for spirit and Earth.
What if peace on Earth begins at birth?

# △
# MYSTICAL EXPERIENCES

A mystical experience is a moment of profound connection with the Spirit of Life. I believe there are two types: consciousness-shifting mystical experiences, which trigger a spiritual awakening, and non-consciousness-shifting mystical experiences, which bring us into a sense of awe and interconnectedness with the Spirit of Life but don't trigger a significant or lasting awakening.

A mystical experience has a beginning and an end. A spiritual awakening is a gradual, unfolding process that leaves us forever changed and changing, for once we're on it, the awakening journey never ends, and our consciousness continues to deepen as more and more of us comes online.

As we travel deeper into our spiritual awakening, there may be times when things seem more active and we're more 'awake,' but these are just different parts of the awakening process as our soul is invited to incarnate deeper than before and our consciousness is invited to expand alongside it. We may have several different stages of awakening on our spiritual journey (see *The Ascent: Awakening of the Mind, Heart, and Body* on page 15 and *The Descent: The Dark Nights of the Soul* on page 20) and generally these are triggered by consciousness-shifting mystical experiences.

In 2009, a survey by the Pew Research Center in the USA found that almost 50 percent of respondents had had a religious or mystical experience. While some mystical experiences may be utterly show-stopping and life-changing, others can be subtle, subliminal, and gentle.

*A mystical experience is a moment when the horizontal (spirit, heaven) and vertical (physical, Earth) meet.*

## When we attune to the sacred and our soul lands more fully into our body.

Mind, body, and spirit harmonize, and we step into what the ancient Greeks called *kairos* time (as opposed to *chronos*, or chronological time). *Kairos* time is sacred time, soul time. It's where the mystical resides, where our intuition lands in our lap, where all creativity happens. Often there's an experience of unity, and our sense of self is replaced by a feeling of oneness or merging with the Spirit of Life. Another term I use for a mystical experience is a unitive experience, as we shift from the separate linear to the unitive whole. Time appears to expand as we drop fully into the present moment.

## CONSCIOUSNESS-SHIFTING MYSTICAL EXPERIENCES

This type of mystical experience deeply changes us. Once you've had one, you can't go back. You're not the same person. It's a moment when you can't unsee what's been seen – perhaps outwardly or inwardly. Something within you has awoken.

Some people say that through their consciousness-shifting mystical experiences, they receive some sort of wisdom, knowing, or clarity about Life itself. Another common observation is that it's difficult to convey the extent of the mystical experience – while it's been felt and known, words are simply too limited to describe it.

I'll never forget the consciousness-shifting mystical experience I had while flying to Australia after hearing my friend Blair was in a coma. I was in that lucid dreaming state between wakefulness and sleep when I physically felt his presence on my body. I felt him embrace me, and in that moment, I knew his soul was gone from this world.

This experience changed the trajectory of my life. Blair and I had always said that we'd answer the call to write a book together once we'd reached the pinnacles of our respective careers – mine as a creative director, his as an actor. Soon after his death, assisted by the deepest grief I'd ever felt, I gathered up the courage to create an escape plan to quit my job and write my book. That book was *Light Is the New Black* and I dedicated it to Blair.

Over the years I've been blessed to hear and hold accounts of mystical experiences that have triggered awakenings in others. A friend told me of the peace and clarity that descended as she sat at the bedside of her dying grandmother. And the sense of being 'spoken through' as her nan took her final breaths, and she prayed her out of this world. I recall her searching for the words to describe how time had stood still, the energy in the room had shifted, and it felt as if they were both being held by something unseen.

Another friend shared an experience that arrived through meditation. On the last day of a long silent retreat, he was feeling a bit disheartened and as if he'd made 'no progress,' when out of nowhere, he physically felt a surge of compassion enter his body. It moved down through the top of his head and with a slow pressure continued through his body and into the ground. Once the force had gone, my friend instantly wept tears of beauty. He felt he'd been shown an embodied understanding of pure love.

It's important to clarify that some consciousness-shifting mystical experiences can require support and integration because they change us so deeply. Perhaps the consciousness shifts so dramatically that our identity changes, or the experience causes such a reconnection with the Spirit of Life that it brings up all that's unlike it. I strongly encourage professional help and guidance when needed, although in my own experience that can be difficult to find. It's my dream that our world changes in such a way that we can see, understand, and support those through the awakening process and treat them with deep respect, devotion, and honor.

A friend shared an experience she had at a conference while a fellow delegate spoke of important but disturbing facts about historical atrocities perpetrated against women. She was instantly  o v e r c o m e  by a deep sense of ancient rage, her entire being humming with white-hot anger. It arose out of nowhere, but it was deeply physical and made her cry big, hot, fast tears. She felt she was experiencing the suffering of all the women who'd ever been and were yet to come. It was powerful and revelatory, but also excruciating, and it took her a long time to make sense of it.

In fact, that same experience returned to my friend many years later, but then, recognizing it, she felt able to receive it differently, to hold that energy differently. This is an important example of the truth that difficult doesn't always mean bad. And when we have the awareness and tools to handle these experiences as they arise, we can continue the work of integrating them into our life and into our relationships. We can extract the lessons, the wisdom, the insight, and carry them differently.

I share this with the intention of connecting you with your mystical experiences – perhaps ones you've had but didn't identify as such at the time – and inviting your awareness to receive them in the future. In our busy lives, it's easy to overlook or dismiss a mystical experience. Whether it's hearing a voice, feeling a knowing, seeing a symbolic shape in nature, being contacted by that long-lost friend you dreamed about, sensing time stretch... Stop doubting it. We know our minds are skilled at dismissing what they can't logically understand or explain, but perhaps this too is part of the practice – what happens when we lean in a little more to those small moments that take our breath away?

## SOUL INQUIRY

*Have you had a consciousness-shifting mystical experience? What did it shift in you?*

# △
# AWE AND WONDER

When each of us was born, we were in a state of wonder and awe. Awake. All babies and young children are. Open-hearted and open-minded, the world was our playground. We saw the magic of Life and the breathtaking, interconnected beauty of nature. Fascinated by flowers and leaves, blades of grass, clouds, and trees. I wonder, could we all then see the Unseen Spirit of Life?

Somewhere along the way, most of us became disconnected from this state of being, cut off from seeing the sacred in all living things. We realized we were separate and formed our own unique identity. We started looking back to the past and into the future. Maybe we got hurt or maybe we just took on the conditioning of the world around us.

Past and future rip us from the sweet, honeyed nectar of Life. The present moment is where life-force is in full potency. Where the Spirit of Life is fully present. And if we're fully present to it, we'll experience it too. We cling on to anything that will ease the pain of this separation and hunger to be reconnected with it. And all the ways that we try to avoid pain disconnect us more and more from the present moment and from the intelligent pulse of life.

But we can return to it in any given moment. Life-force is waiting for us there. The best way to return to it is to enter a state of awe and wonder, and the easiest way to do that is to truly be in nature and notice the beauty that's waiting for you there in the present moment. You'll return to your true nature when you do. Awe and wonder are two of the most powerful states for the mystic and they're the quickest way to have a direct experience of the Spirit of Life. And when you reconnect with that, you reconnect with your soul. When you reconnect with your soul you reconnect with life-force and remember who you are and why you chose to come to this life.

> **When we allow ourselves to experience awe, we feel a sense of immanence and transcendence at the same time. Heaven and Earth connect. Spirit and matter weave together. Soul comes online.**

When we activate a state of awe and wonder we open ourselves to having a mystical experience. A unitive experience. We become one with the rest of life and feel less alone. We experience a moment of peace, awakening, and connection. A shift in consciousness and an expansion can occur. It can be both subtle and significant; regardless, the soul comes a little more fully into the body and mind, and heart, body, and soul align with the rest of life.

The easiest way I know to have a mystical experience is to consciously choose to be in a state of awe and wonder while observing the world. It's as if time both stretches and doesn't exist. There's room to breathe and we feel in communion with and connected to everything around us. When we allow ourselves to enter a state of awe in the moment we experience true communion with Life. When we experience communion with Life, we also experience communion with ourselves. We remember our own true nature by truly being in the moment. In nature. In our own true nature.

I remember the first time I was conscious of having entered a state of awe and wonder. I'd just got my driver's license and was dropping a friend home; as I took the coastal road, which wound around a headland between two beaches, I caught a glimpse in my rearview mirror of the sun setting over the ocean. My breath was taken and all I could say (to myself) was, 'Wow!' The experience would reoccur whenever I subsequently reached this point on my drive, and each time it felt like my heart expanded and my soul landed more fully in my body.

You don't need to be spiritual to see the sacred and experience awe every day. Each night my dad sits on the balcony and watches as the great Australian sky is painted in oranges, pinks, and purples. He might not consider himself a spiritual man, but he enters a state of awe more times than most through this nightly ritual.

I lived on a busy street in Glastonbury that was on the Mary ley line, and so hundreds of pilgrims would pass by it each day. It had a magnificent garden that contained the most exquisite honeysuckle bush that ran along the fence. One of my favorite things to do was to watch people as they walked past the honeysuckle. Some would race by and miss it, focused only on their destination; others would make the honeysuckle communion part of their daily walk.

Then there were those who would walk past and suddenly be stopped in their tracks. If they allowed it, these people were the most delighted of all – they would lean over and drink in the sweet honey scent. It was visible, the shift that occurred. It was as if they experienced a quick realignment, a dropping in, a slowing down and a deepening, as for just a second or two they would enter a state of awe by being with the delicious beauty of nature and reconnecting with the Spirit of Life.

In the moments after having my son, as I began to process the details of the birth, I looked down at him and all of a sudden, I was generally surprised to find a baby in my arms. This response perplexed me for such a long time afterward. I remember saying to my therapist, 'I don't understand why I was so surprised to see him there. I knew I was having a baby, so why did I react like that?' She replied: 'But how is anyone to react when a miracle occurs right before their eyes?' Awe at the great mystery of life.

## SOUL INQUIRY

*Can you recall having moments of awe in nature or any mystical experiences?*

# △
# BECOMING AN AWE SEEKER

*'If you truly love nature, you will find beauty everywhere.'*

VINCENT VAN GOGH

Entering a state of awe and wonder is easy if you try. In fact, it requires no real effort at all. Two things are required: first, that you notice and appreciate the beauty that's around you: a flower, a tree, a sunset, a sleeping baby, falling leaves, a bird singing, a river flowing, a fire flickering; and second, that you slow down and allow yourself to be present and merge with nature by fully receiving the beauty of the moment. You witness the sacred that's already here. This practice of seeking moments of awe is one that we use in The Inner Temple Mystery School, and I've observed how truly life-changing it can be. So often we miss seeing the sacred that's already here, all around us.

I think one of the reasons why nature evokes a state of awe in us is the harmonious beauty it possesses. And as we see the sacred that's here, something harmonizes within us and the sacred within us is remembered too. This is the moment when the soul lands fully in our body, and it's as if heaven and Earth meet. We feel both connected with all of Life *and* so insignificant in the vastness and wonder of it all.

Words fail us. We're captivated by the present moment. Time stands still or gets stretchy. *Kairos* time, mystical sacred time, is activated. And when that happens, we're able to feel true joy. We're able to hear our intuition clearly. Ideas come in fully formed. We regulate to the pulse of Life, and we enter a state of receiving and healing (wholeness).

Becoming an awe seeker opens both your heart and your mind. Becoming an awe seeker connects you with the secrets of the cosmos as the ordered Universe. You're part of this beautiful, harmonious order. Becoming an awe seeker soothes the ache of the separation that so many of us feel. Becoming an awe seeker gives you a way of finding peace in the moment, wherever you are. Becoming an awe seeker is the gateway to walking your sacred path.

## SOUL INQUIRY

*Go into nature and see if you can shift into a state of awe.*
*Do it for 10 seconds if you like. Take 10 big breaths*
*and see if you can truly be in the present moment.*
*Notice the beauty around you, and consciously*
*choose to connect with the Spirit of Life.*
*Notice the shift that occurs and journal about your experience.*

# △
# JOY IS HERE IF YOU WANT IT

The place where life-force is bountiful is in the present moment. The place where joy is found is in the present moment. The place where creativity resides is in the present moment. The place where intuition waits for you is in the present moment. Fear and resentment about the past and worries and projections about the future cut us off from our joy because they cut us off from the Spirit of Life.

If you're thinking of the past or worrying about the future, you're not in alignment with the force of Life. You're disconnected in that moment. Micromanaging the great intelligence instead of claiming it as you. Relying on your personal will over the great mystery itself. You don't need to spend all day in the present moment, but the more time you spend here, the more in alignment you'll feel.

And the good news is that at any moment of any day you can bring yourself into the present moment. You can choose to break through the illusion of the past and future and drink in the sweet nectar of Life whenever you wish. This is why spiritual practices – from dancing to chanting to meditating – are so effective: they are gateways for the soul to drop fully in. However, anything that works with the senses invites the soul to come in: poetry, song, sex, delicious food. In these moments we find ourselves in the center of heaven and Earth. Soul drops into the physical and everything expands. Spirit and matter build a bridge through the connection.

## SOUL INQUIRY

*How can you open yourself up to experiencing joy right now?*

△

# THE DIFFERENCE BETWEEN BEAUTY AND PERFECTION

Life is beautiful. But it isn't pretty. Beauty is very different from pretty. Pretty is perfect, but it's static, fixed, paper-thin. It holds no substance; it has no depth; and it's not really alive. Pretty never lasts, but beauty is timeless. Beauty holds the essence of Life; it contains within it the great mystery and the extremes – the ecstasy and the agony. Beauty is made up of polarity. Beauty takes the breath away and transforms the beholder through its brutal honesty; it activates the breath of life as they exhale in awe, and this brings them into the present moment.

Birth and death are beautiful; love is beautiful; friendship is beautiful; growth is beautiful. All things that are beautiful have a tension in them. Perhaps it's this tension that makes them beautiful, for we appreciate how much of a blessing and a miracle they are when we witness them in their fleeting state in that never-to-be-seen-again moment. Babies are beautiful, flowers are beautiful, the ocean is beautiful, life is beautiful.

I'd much rather be beautiful than pretty, for pretty will always fade. Beauty will always deepen, through all the seasons, while pretty is only about being pretty.

*Beauty is much more than appearance.*
*It's a vibration, a harmony, a truth. Beauty*
*always has a deeper purpose.*

If you open your eyes, you'll see that this world is made up of such beauty. And if you do your best to acknowledge it when you can, you'll instantly be brought into the present moment. And you'll be inspired to embrace your true nature and sacred purpose, for it's the fact that all things change that makes them all the more beautiful in that moment.

Any parent of young children will tell you how the minute they think they've got the hang of the way things are, everything changes. Those early years are so precious and they're also, in most cases, so difficult. They go so fast, and they also drag on and on. One moment you want the time to slow down and in the next, you want it to get easier and speed up. And one of the greatest challenges is to embrace the polarity of this beauty all at once. This is the great mystery of life.

## SOUL INQUIRY

*How are you seeking perfection or prettiness over beauty?*

*How can you embrace beauty a little bit more?*

# △
# BECOMING A BEAUTY SEEKER

For me, beauty is harmony. My mother was my first teacher when it came to beauty. A Virgo like me, she has a knack of making everything she touched beautiful. Decades later, in my work as a creative director, I learned a great deal about art direction, but it wasn't until I stepped into my devotional work that I truly understood beauty as a way of life.

When I first started working with my publisher and other third parties, I felt that I was being difficult due to my perfectionism when it came to the aesthetics of my creations. Then one day I realized that creating beauty is a devotional practice and it happens both in the seen and unseen worlds. Now, whenever I collaborate with anyone, I explain that to work with me they need to understand this! With the reframe, it's amazing how easily people get it.

Aesthetic beauty is the most understood form of beauty. Essentially, it's the visual beauty of something, and it brings into play such things as color, symmetry, and other physical attributes. Natural beauty tends to encapsulate beauty in the natural world, such as landscapes, sunsets, a starlit sky, all of which evoke a sense of awe and wonder.

Artistic beauty refers to creations such as art, poetry, music, and dance. Things created by artists that call up different feeling states in the beholder. The artist has merged with the sacred and created something that didn't exist before.

Geometric beauty is all about harmony and sacred order. This is the beauty that we see echoed throughout nature and it's why being in nature can return us to our own true nature. The golden ratio, the ultimate harmonious proportion, is an example of this kind of beauty; found throughout nature, it's also used to create art, buildings, and other physical objects, which is why these things often captivate us so much.

Energetic beauty is about what's unseen. A different form of harmony and sacred order, it's the most misunderstood type of beauty. It can be sensed but not touched. When I create sacred spaces, this is the main form of beauty I'm working with. I also work with energetic beauty when writing a book. First, the words are put on the page, but then, I go through the text two, three, maybe four times and energetically cut back anything that doesn't quite land right. I do this while playing devotional music and sometimes I even chant. I also have an altar for the book, which I tend even after the book's left my arms.

The seen and unseen beauty of my physical surroundings has always been especially important to me, and as I've grown and deepened in my career, the aesthetic beauty of my creations and the harmony in my writing remain a priority. Before I teach a workshop, I always spend time in the space beforehand, making it beautiful for the group to be held. As I move things physically and aesthetically and bring in different objects from nature and other places, I'm activating the sacred container for the group. I'm also shifting the energy and creating harmony; you'll see me pottering about, setting up altars and arranging sacred objects like my oracle cards until it all feels just right. I do this in most areas of my life, including in my home.

## SOUL INQUIRY

*How are you being called to create more*
*beauty in your surroundings today?*

△

# RETURNING TO THE WISDOM WITHIN

In the modern world of spirituality there are numerous tools designed to keep us wanting more, more, more, and these can both help and hinder us. However, to connect with God or Goddess or the Spirit of Life, we don't *need* spiritual tools. The connection, the bridge, with the sacred is you, and you can always go direct. Your heart is the portal to more wisdom than you'll ever be able to seek outside of yourself. But to connect with your heart, you need it to be open.

Recently a guest on my podcast confessed that she'd become dependent on oracle cards, crystals, and connecting with unseen external sources (such as angels and guides) for guidance. She'd stopped trusting her own intuition or inner connection because she felt she needed these tools or outer intermediaries, and as a result, had put her tools aside. If you've become dependent on external sources to connect with your intuition or the sacred, this is what I want you to know:

You have everything you need within you to go direct. Your heart is the gateway to it all. When I was in my twenties, one of my teachers, Sonia Choquette, taught me to place my hand on my heart to connect with my intuition and then just say what feels true in my heart. So, anytime you're questioning things or find yourself seeking answers outside of yourself, you can always return to the sacred and the wisdom within through the portal of your heart. It will never fail you and it's always available to guide you.

It's important to know that you have it all within you. All people do. But we're living in times when we've not been taught how to connect with our heart as our main newsfeed. And while all the external tools out there are gateways to support you in connecting with your innate wisdom and the sacred that's within you, the sacred isn't separate from you. The wisdom is and always will be waiting for you deep within.

### All you need to do to connect with the sacred is connect with yourself through the portal of your heart.

The reason I love working with nature as a guide is because it doesn't have a mind, so it cannot get stuck in the past or think about the future. It simply is what it is. It embraces the truth in the moment in every single moment. It knows how to BE. It hurtles along with the sacred pulse of Life. And because it's so aligned to this pulse, because it embraces the life-force that's essentially spiritual energy, it invites us into this sacred present moment too, by being in it.

I believe that when we're in this sacred present moment we're able to reconnect with both life-force (the sacred, intelligent pulse of Life) and our own being-ness. And when we reconnect with our own being-ness we drop into our bodies and our hearts. Mind, body, soul become aligned. And with this alignment our intuition can speak and be heard, seen, and known.

I think this happens in two ways. Firstly, we're able to connect with what's true for us, and secondly, through connecting with our own truth we're also able to connect with a universal truth. For we're all part of the organism of Life. So, when you're working with guides, whether in the physical or spiritual, always use them as gateways, as doors for you to connect with the sacred that's always been and always will be within. This is where your intuition resides. This is where your inner wisdom lies. This is where God is. Because God isn't an external being separate from you. The sacred is and always has been seeded and waiting for you within.

If while working with nature as a guide you receive wisdom or information that feels slightly different from just your intuition, it may be wisdom from nature itself for the collective. Now, this doesn't mean you need to do anything with this wisdom – you can also just receive it for yourself. Right now, the Earth and humanity are healing after a long separation. From each other and the sacred. And so, when we connect with nature as a guide, we may receive messages from the trees, the waters, the flowers, and beyond. I believe these messages are us healing with the Earth, returning to the Earth.

## SOUL INQUIRY

*What is the wisdom within you wanting you to know?*

Her grandmother's grandmother's
wisdom was etched into the stones.
Waiting for the time to come when her
daughter's daughter would have
the ears to hear it.

*my grandmother is calling me* △

# △
# THE INVITATION

There's no denying it, as a planet we're going through something. After being focused for too long on our separation and individualism, it's clear that this old way of being must die. That humanity must come together. Our survival depends on it.

I believe we're living through a period of evolution and that humanity is being given a choice: continue living in our separate ways and face destruction or reconnect with the Spirit of Life and creation. Death is certain. Rebirth is an option – but we must wake up to choose it. We must open our hearts to choose it. Our evolution depends on it. Nothing is certain.

*I believe our planetary Mother is urging us to say yes to creation, not destruction. To return to the Earth, ourselves, and each other.*

If we say yes to creation, we say yes to death with a rebirth. It's nature's way. If we say yes to destruction, will we be walking toward our own extinction? Is the Great Mother waking us up from our unconscious slumber in a bid to make us choose? Is she trying to open our eyes, our hearts, and our minds to how our unconscious ways have caused such harm to each other and the planet? How unaligned to Life itself we've become?

Are we in the birth canal for a new way forward for humanity? Is this the darkest night before the morn? Will we align ourselves with the intelligent pulse of Life before it's too late? Will humanity be included in the evolution of the Earth? Is this why the Great Mother is appearing in the hearts of so many?

Are the grief, pain, and agony that so many of us are facing proof that we're an interconnected species? Is what we're feeling and purging and processing the key to returning to our evolution? Are we the midwives and the mothers and the children of a new humanity? Is this why we chose to come? Do you remember why you chose to come?

## SOUL INQUIRY

*If the Earth were to speak to you right now, what would it say?*

# △
# FUTURE ANCESTORS OF THE EARTH

It's our disconnection from the Earth that makes us feel like orphans. Like motherless souls. Wherever you are, acknowledge the Earth and its keepers. The ancestors and custodians through the ages who have tended the sacred Earth that lies beneath you. And also those who contributed to its decline. It's difficult to acknowledge that our ancestors may have been involved in the severing, but true healing can only happen when we allow ourselves to do so.

In acknowledging the history of the planet beneath us we're able to return to the Earth and thus reconnect with the Spirit of Life and receive its holding and belonging. We can begin to heal what's been severed and open the pathways of healing for those to come after us. When we start to clear and reactivate our connection with our Great Mother Earth, we return to her arms. We're the new Earth keepers. The deactivators and the activators. The ones called forth by ancestors future and past to choose a different way.

May we find the courage to open our hearts and mend what's been broken, taken, ignored, unacknowledged, silenced, dismissed, bound, and forgotten. As hard as it may be, may we choose to heal the disconnection and severing that we've inherited, regardless of whose fault it is. May we choose the path of healing. Of rethreading. Of reweaving. Of listening to the Earth's ancient and future song and be led.

## SOUL INQUIRY

*How are you being called to be a positive*
*ancestor of those yet to come?*

The land is here for us
The stones are here for us.
The air is here for us.
The trees are here for us.

The flowers are here for us.
The weeds are here for us.
The mountains are here for us.
The rivers are here for us.

The oceans are here for us.
The mushrooms are here for us.
The animals are here for us.
The children are here for us.

When will we remember
how to be there for them?

*soul loss* △

# △
# CODES OF THE
# WILDFLOWERS AND THE WEEDS

They told me I had to go to the store to buy what I needed. Consume not create. But no matter what I reached for, I was always left hungry. Ravenous. Feeling that I could never quite get what I needed. Craved. Hungered for. So many years spent numbing myself while my mitochondria longed for nourishment and a connection with my grandmother's grandmother's grandmother's wisdom and lineages lost, drowned, bound, and burned.

These weeds, these wild native wildflowers and weeds. These nourishing plant elders that ancient ones tended. Grandmothers and grandfathers since the beginning of time. I was taught to order them online, with a click, from places foreign, wondering why they did not satiate or speak. Lost in translation. Aching for a harmonious constellation.

Perfectly cut, dried, and packaged. Unable to reach the marrow. Consuming but not absorbing. My body unable to access what it most needed; yearning for the key to open the cell doors. Missing the repetitive embodiment of generations ancient. Bending, tending, cultivating. I watch my toddler mimicking my movements, hands in the earth, and see now that this physical, emotional, spiritual, existential yearning runs deep. He sees the Spirit of Life. Like attracts like.

These wildflowers, these wild native weeds. These nourishing herbs that ancient ones tended. Grandmothers and grandfathers, wise ones, healers. Track me all the way back to the Original Mother. It took me so many years to discover that this whole time they were at my door. Growing through the cracks in the paving stones. Nettle and dandelion, marigold and mugwort, stubbornly blasting their way through the harsh cement. Fighting their way through.

So misunderstood, so overlooked. Forbidden, hunted, cut back and cut out, discarded, burned, poisoned, and banished. All because of their wildness. Their song fading from our ears but felt by our hearts through our longing for something untamed. But I can hear the Ancient Grandmothers of the Earth now. My inner ear open to the whispers. My inner eye refocused on the unseen before me.

We were taught that beauty was perfection. That we must grow in rows. To be forever in bloom. That we'd be discarded if we didn't. Grow, grow, grow. Don't step out of line. Cling on to those petals. Withstand every winter, fall, and storm. Fruit, fruit, fruit. No wonder we've grown weary. No wonder there's barely any wild left within.

And still the nourishment is on offer to us near and deep. This whole time, the wildflowers and the weeds have continued to grow before us. And for us. They were pulled up and replaced with perfect, manicured, identical rows, but each attempt to eradicate them only made them grow stronger. Fiercer. These resilient, nourishing weeds are our ancestors past. The ones who couldn't be silenced and snuffed out. Cultivated and watered down.

Yes, these weeds are the seeds of the ones they tried to bury. And they remind us that we are too. Defying all odds. Beckoning us both back and forth from lineages lost. To reach all the way back so that together we can go forward and plant ourselves more fully here than ever before. I pray that it be. May we return to the wild Earth.

## SOUL INQUIRY

*If the wildflowers were to speak to you*
*right now, what would they say?*

# △
## SLOWING DOWN TO THE PACE OF THE EARTH

The mind and the soul have a speed of their own. Especially for those of us who come in with a particular soul mission. And especially those whose mission feels time dependent. Which is perhaps all of us. It's easy to burn out. To feel like time's running out. And it is running out. But not in the way that we think. Time's running out for us to slow down. To reconnect with the Spirit of Life and sync back in with the cycles of the Earth.

The urgency we may feel is both true and false. True in that we must wake up and slow down to the pace of the Earth. False in that toxic capitalism has got us so out of sync with the rhythm of the Earth that we've been hypnotized into a state of urgency, emergency, and dysregulation. It's something that we inherited, and we must wake up to it before it's too late. For us, not the Earth. For the Earth will find her way. The question is, will humanity?

Your presence here matters. The potency of your energy and life-force matters. Play the long game, not the short one. Your soul chose to be here, on this planet, at this time, in this body, and while you're here, you form part of the Earth's cycles and rhythms.

If you resist the ebb and flow of nature, the intelligent pulse, the ever-changing seasons (inner and outer), you'll be made to slow down eventually. Whether through burnout or disconnection from your life-force. So many of us are hurting right now. Experiencing the deep healing that's required of us as a species. So many of us are processing the sickness of our society and culture being so disconnected from the Spirit of Life.

Don't underestimate the rebellious act that is reconnecting with the Spirit of Life. Don't underestimate the revolutionary act of slowing down to the pace of the Earth. Don't underestimate the ability of nature and Life to find creative solutions. And because you are part of nature and part of Life, be open to being a vessel for those solutions.

When you reconnect with the Spirit of Life and let it move through you, you're walking your sacred path. This is the way of the mystic. This is living in alignment with the intelligent pulse of Life. When you feel as if you're not doing enough, when you tell yourself that it's not okay to rest, know that you hold a thread for the healing of humanity.

*Slowing down, regulating our nervous systems, in a world that's stuck in a state of emergency is a revolutionary act.*

Regulating our nervous systems will heal more than we could ever imagine, for when we do so, we reconnect with the Great Mother's heartbeat. We become a safe haven to which others can flock and co-regulate. The more we ignore the warning signs to slow down, the more brittle we'll become and the more we'll need to rely on things and substances outside of our true nature just to survive, let alone thrive.

It's no secret that the Earth's out of balance right now because of humanity. I also believe it's out of balance because we've forgotten the sacred laws of the Earth. The sacred laws of Life. The sacred laws of the cosmos. Because we've forgotten or been disconnected from the sacred, rhythmic pulse of this planet. Of nature itself. Which is why, by reconnecting with nature and its cycles we can find our way back to a state of balance, both for ourselves and the planet.

The Earth itself, without humanity, knows how to regenerate, recorrect, rebalance, replenish, rebirth. The Earth wants to support us in remembering that we know how to do this too. It will regulate you if you let it. It will nourish you if you let it. It will replenish you if you let it. But there will come a point when, if we don't wake up to it, it will be too late. This is also the urgency many of us feel. But don't mistake it for the other urgency.

## SOUL INQUIRY

*At what speed are you currently traveling?*

*What's one thing you can do to slow down to the pace of the Earth?*

# △
# ATTRACTING LIKE A FLOWER

Have you ever noticed how in summer, when the roses are at their fullest and their scent is hanging in the air, bees and other pollinators suddenly appear? Roses don't run all over the place reaching and grabbing; instead, they rely on the bees to come to them. The rose is never grasping for the bee. It's never o    v    e    r    s    t    r    e    t    c    h    i    n    g. It embraces what it is fully and allows Life to come to it. It receives it fully. It doesn't open and close according to who walks by; it opens and blooms regardless.

How can you open yourself up to receiving abundance, rose style? How can you fully open yourself up to the sweetness of your life and embrace the magnificence of who you are? And also open yourself up to the possibility of receiving what you yearn for deeply? How can you be clear on what you desire? How can you ask for it? How can you trust that all that's meant for you wants to come to you? How can you state your desires out loud and let your yearnings be known?

Don't reach or grasp; don't strive, control, or manipulate – that will leave you exhausted, parched, and brittle. This chapter is a message that true, sustainable abundance is coming. Connect with your sensual, true nature. Be unashamed of what you desire. And when it comes, relish each minute.

## SOUL INQUIRY

*What do you really desire?*

*What are you ready to open yourself up to receive?*

*How can you attract like a flower?*

# △
# BE PRODUCTIVE, DO NOTHING

You can stretch time when you're truly still. You can reconnect with the Spirit of Life simply by creating some space. Just because you're not 'doing something,' it doesn't mean nothing's being done. Sometimes more can happen when you don't worry so much about every little thing getting done. The soul dreams of wide empty spaces. It demands room to breathe. Don't cage it, don't fence it in.

When you overschedule your schedule, you suffocate your soul. When you jam too much into your day you disconnect from the Spirit of Life. When you feel trapped, your creativity is stifled and what once was a co-creation becomes a production. When you produce, you rely on your own, exhaustive ways. When you create you become a muse for the Spirit of Life. And in turn, life-force is breathed through you.

Open your arms, heart, and schedule wide enough for your soul to occupy and land into your day. Without space, nothing new can drop in. Without space, nothing unexpected can tap you on the shoulder. Without space, there's no co-creation and no room for grace. You're one cell in a larger creative cosmic organism. Life is creative and because you're part of it you're creative too. Leave space for the creative pulse of Life to dream with and through you.

The Universe is self-organizing, which means when we stop trying to bend it to our own personal will, it frees itself to get to work on our behalf. Anyone who manages a team of people knows that micromanaging others sends the message that you don't trust them to do their jobs. You're running everything through you. It's not sustainable and eventually you'll burn out. This is a difficult one to get in our overly individualistic society.

Life is like this too. If you don't trust it to work for you while you sleep or do something else, you'll stop it from being able to surprise and delight you. If you think that the intelligent pulse of Life needs you to be frantically doing in order for anything to be done, then eventually nothing will be done on your behalf.

Imagine the Great Cosmic Mother beating her drum. Do you trust her to keep doing what she's done since the beginning of time? What if we learned to leave space for Life to support us, to surprise us? Sometimes the most productive thing you can do is loosen your grip on the way things should be, and trust in the fruits yet to come.

## SOUL INQUIRY

*How can you create more space in your life?*

*What makes your soul feel free?*

*What makes your soul feel trapped?*

# △
# YOU'RE NOT NORMAL, AND THAT'S NORMAL

No two soul paths are the same. Your soul came here against all odds into a body, onto a planet, into a lineage, at a time like no other that ever was or will again be. You're not normal, and that's normal.

Nature needs diversity in order to thrive and survive, and mind, body, soul, we need it too. Somewhere along the way we decided it was best to try to fit in, to endeavor to be normal. But normal isn't natural. Normal is manufactured, produced. Normal isn't sustainable. Diversify or die – this is what nature teaches us.

The moment we try to grow in perfect little rows is the moment we find ourselves disconnected from the intelligent pulse of Life in its potency. We lose a bit of life-force every time we do attempt to fit in. The tall poppy knows, the weeds do too. We were never meant to grow in rows, in the same way at the same time. To be like everyone else.

*We came here to be soul embodied.*
*Spirit woven into matter.*
*The miraculous unseen manifested into form.*

Against all odds, we managed to be here. Each of us has been on a huge journey to be here – a unique, multifaceted soul in a unique ancestry at a unique time. Every breath, every moment in the endless trajectory of your soul's journey, each imprinting and curating the most exquisite, unique form.

No two ancestries are the same. No two lands are the same. No two life conditions are the same. No two times are the same. And so no two soul paths are the same. You're not normal, and that's normal. You were never meant to fit in.

## SOUL INQUIRY

*How are you trying to fit in?*

*How can you embrace who you truly are a little bit more?*

△

# DON'T PUT THEM ON A PEDESTAL

If you've elevated a person to a godly level, turn around and kiss your own feet. We've all done it, but it results in more separation, unnecessary projections, and hefty, unfair falls. Because if you're to step into your power and grow, and you *are* here to grow, anyone that you position above yourself will eventually need to be cut down.

Be kind to them and to you: don't put them on a pedestal in the first place. That way, you'll never have to cut them down. And if you have positioned someone above you, take responsibility by letting what you admire in them rise on up within you, right alongside them.

Respect, reverence, and inspiration are different from idolization. You don't need someone else to fall in order to claim who you truly are. Let the tall poppy be. If you cut it down, you'll likely be cut down too. Instead, let them remind you that what you worship in another is wanting to be tended and encouraged within you too. Water those seeds with your love and attention and someday soon they'll flower and then they'll fruit.

## SOUL INQUIRY

*Who have you put on a pedestal in the past or currently?*

*What did you/do you admire in them?*

*How can you nurture or embody that within you without cutting them down?*

# △
# A SHIFT TO POTENCY
# AND SIMPLICITY

We're going through a period of great healing and great change. Along with the planet, you're rebuilding who you are from mind to cell. Your heart needs to be at the center of it all. And when you gather the courage to live in this way, you dream a new world into form. This is the vessel for your soul's dream to be felt before it's known.

The path of the mystic is the path of the heart, and in following it you join forces with a lineage of sacred dreamers who came before. At a time when all external structures and systems are crumbling, this is really all that remains. The path of the heart is the steadiest there is.

Your heart was the first organ to be woven into matter. When it stops beating your soul will have lost its form. When we trust the path of the heart, we stop trying to figure it all out and instead shift into living into the present moment. When we live into the present moment, the next right step is always revealed.

When we're with someone we deeply love, it seems as if everything stands still. Our nervous system co-regulates with theirs and we feel held, seen, and safe. This is the state that's best for us. This is the state where all healing happens and where our soul's wisdom resides. But we don't need anyone or anything to access this state. When we drop into this space, we align ourselves with the pulse of Life. And when we do that, our life-force replenishes, and our soul can drop more fully into the physical.

If you endeavor to spend more time in this space, all will expand for you. Your worldly striving will fall away and be replaced by proper attraction. People will feel the heart expanse that you transmit. Let that be your calling card.

> *You'll be rewarded for simplicity. You'll be praised for potent authenticity. Be the creative, the human, the mystic, be the dreamer.*

The days of hustle, exhaustion, and producing over creating are coming to an end. Those who choose potency over mass production, heart over head, slow over overdrive, will lead in this new era. Release all the time-wasting, energy-wasting, resource-wasting parts of your life. While in the past they may have got you ahead, now as we enter this new quickening paradigm they'll become less and less productive and effective. The Earth is making sure of it. Anything that's unsustainable will not flourish. This is the new law of the Earth.

If you succumb to merely feeding the machine, you'll waste the seeds you came here to plant. Sing your heart to the vast black velvet sky. Don't leave here with any of it still in you. Peel back the unnecessary outgoings. Keep things potent and free. Your energy, your life-force, your love, your time are the most valuable forces. Protect them and treat them like the precious resources they are. This is how you'll acquire true wealth. This is how you'll flourish. This is how you'll receive deep soul satisfaction. This is how to truly live.

## SOUL INQUIRY

*What in your life is overcomplicated and unnecessary? How can you make things a little simpler?*

*Where in your life are you leaking energy? What can you free yourself from that's exhausting you the most?*

*What makes you feel truly abundant and free?*

# △
# FREE MY WILD MYSTIC HEART

I long to connect, not perfect. To create, not produce. To dream, not be certain. To wonder, not convince. I'm a mystic, not a machine. I need space to explore, to question, to dream a new dream. I need my questions to give birth to more questions, not be trapped by certain answers.

Certainty is death without rebirth. So, hurl me into the fertile void of the winter deep and dark. For I know that the end is also the beginning and that the brightest dawn comes after the darkest night.

Change is creation. Only those who dream of the unfathomable will ever be able to create anything truly new. So, I take my feet off the factory floor. My soul knows I don't need more, more, more. That isn't what I'm truly hungry for. Show me how to find my ground, no matter where I'm planted.

Even through the cracks in the sidewalk, I'll find a way to break free of the cage of the ordinary. Don't fence me in. Free my wild mystic heart. Replant me where the wildflowers grow. Yes, take me to where I can roam free, where I can keep my heart open front and back.

Where there's room to breathe. Where the sting is sometimes the antidote to the wound. Where the nectar is always found in the center. Where the hum of the bee reminds my wild mystic heart that I've always been free to be me.

## SOUL INQUIRY

*What does your wild heart most long to do?*

# △
# CREATING VS. PRODUCING:
# MYSTIC VS. MACHINE

We're creative beings living in a creative world. Life itself is creative and it's always creating, every moment of every day. And because you are part of Life, you are always creating too. Many people believe that they're not creative, but to be alive is to be creative. To create is to put things together for something new to be born. A moment earlier, that creation didn't exist, and then all of a sudden, the dream is realized. What an amazing thing creativity is.

However, when we use our creativity for a controlled outcome, it can easily lose the magic and turn into producing. Producing starves the soul. It turns the mystic into a machine. This is the challenge for the artist, for the mystic – to create, not produce. The mystic creates, the machine produces. Anyone can produce pretty much anything if they try. No one can create quite like you.

I believe creativity comes from the soul merging with the Spirit of Life. The urge to create is at our core, but it's our fear and thinking that stop us from doing what's in our true creative nature. To create, you need an open mind and heart, for if they are closed you can't dream of new possibilities. You can't dream at all.

Perhaps it's our rigid adulting ways that stop us from creating solutions that would change the trajectory of this planet's future. Perhaps if we all remembered what it's like to create like children – to dream and play with no attachment to the outcome – the world would be a very different place.

I'm at my happiest when I'm creating, especially if I'm doing so without being attached to a specific outcome. Entering a creative container and asking spirit to move through me and my creations is my idea of bliss. If you're a person whose work is creative, resist being turned into a machine and losing your connection with the spark that inspires you.

> *Our society likes to capitalize what's well received, but we must be careful not to dampen the creative spark that made it possible.*

A few years ago, I felt trapped in my own business. As my work grew and the world of content changed, my team did too. I was increasingly spending time in meetings, focusing on things which, at the end of the day didn't matter, managing people, and producing rather than creating. It felt like I was responding to an external narrative rather than being internally led, which is where the magic is.

My soul felt parched, and like it had no room to breathe. I'd never aspired to 'run a business'; the only reason I'd formed a company was so I could be in devotion sharing my writing and creations as a channel. As my overheads grew, I was working harder and harder and feeling more and more disconnected from the potency of my call. I yearned to be free to create, not produce.

One night I dreamed I was at the bottom of the ocean with a glass dome around me. I deeply longed to swim and explore the deep blue ocean, but I couldn't. The glass dome, which had been built to support me, was stifling me and my connection to spirit and my creativity. I knew that I needed to make some huge changes and so I learned to opt out of the pressure to scale, say yes, and grow, grow, grow. Instead, I prioritized my creativity and connection with spirit above all else, by traveling at my own speed.

In our world of overstimulation, urgency, and content overload, the powers that be will try to get you to produce rather than create. Don't let them. For if you produce for the outcome alone, then the creative well will run dry. You'll disconnect from your soul, and you'll find yourself inside another unsustainable system. The artist creates from the soul and the soul has no motive other than for Life to thrive. Trust the holy, limitless intelligence of your creativity. Resist the machine and say yes to the wildflowers planted deep within.

## SOUL INQUIRY

*In what ways are you producing instead of creating?*

*How are you being called to unhook from a system that's telling you what you should do or that you must keep up with others?*

△

# YOU CAME HERE WITH
# MEDICINE, NOT CANDY

Right now, external forces are calling artists and mystics to produce not create. But you came here with medicine. Don't you remember?

In times like these, it's never been more important to truly create. No artificial thing can compare to the intimacy of the human spirit. Connection is felt in the imperfections of our humanness. In our ability to express that which is felt in the hearts of humanity but has not been expressed.

And so, artists, songwriters, poets, and potters, please don't stop dreaming. Reach high and deep for the seeds and stars that your soul came here with. Don't let the external noise and rapid speed distract you. Trust what's stirring deep in your soul.

Don't just add to the noise. Choose one note, if you have to. That's what will open and harmonize the most hearts. Sing it, sing it, sing it. Honor the potency of what you came here to share. Don't rip it into bite-sized pieces just because you're told that's what the world wants to consume right now, now, now, now. You came here with medicine, not candy.

### *The moment you take direction from the external is the moment you stop dreaming.*

Medicine isn't something that should be consumed lightly. And you came here with medicine, don't you remember? This type of consumption leaves the soul wanting more. Which causes more consumption and separation.

You came here with medicine. Share it in its potency. Anything less would be a waste.

## SOUL INQUIRY

*How are you being called to honor the medicine
you came here with more potently?*

# △
# THE IMAGINAL CELLS

There are many programs in the physical and mental that are stopping us all from progressing. And when I say progressing, I mean becoming less like a linear above or better than, and more like a natural life-force intelligently moving. This intelligent pulse knows what to do, but it does take time. Plants have their phases, and the planet has its seasons, and they manage to move through them without judgment because they have no mind. Humanity, however, has programs driving it from the past and present. But it's possible to unhook from them.

As we each speak our truth and expand through our pain, we're freed from the trance, and our freedom and our voicing of the truth then go on to activate a seed of truth and remembering within another. Dormant dreams awaken from their slumber and awaken dormant dreamers as they dream of possible futures.

The life-force in your mitochondria, while perhaps dormant for centuries, has an intelligence within it which, given the right conditions, knows how to unbind, uncoil, and unfurl. And then there's no stopping what's been started: the uncoiling begins its blueprinted spiral dance to set your soul and lineage free.

*For too long, shame and judgment, fear and pain have run the show. But humanity is taking a turn now. And that's what you came here for.*

You're one of many transformative imaginal cells. As we awaken our souls, we set off a chain of events. Our presence has the potential to awaken all who we meet. It's time for us all to call back that dormant life-force that's been contained and restrained since the Goddess went underground.

Birth isn't pretty. But we're all in the labor of a new humanity. It's what we came here for. We're all wisdom keepers of the Earth. Midwives for each other. Taking turns to contract, surrender, support, and push. No person will be unaffected. Those who resist will continue to struggle. They'll stay in the dark birth canal until they're willing to surrender who they once were and the world they thought they were in.

And those who say yes to the soul's waking dream may feel like they're dying a death. That's because they are. You are too. The end is also the beginning. But before the beginning comes, the Spirit of Life demands that we surrender who we once were for the chance to be born anew. And you came here to birth this world anew. Didn't you?

## SOUL INQUIRY

*What is your soul's deepest dream?*

△

# LIVING YOUR SOUL'S WILD DREAM

Do you know what it took for your soul to be here? Unlock from the systems that attempt to restrain you, scream from the rooftops what sets you free. Let those who try to contain you watch on and take notes. In the grand scheme of the soul, this moment right now doesn't even make it into the highlights.

It's time to break the shackles and set your soul free. To sing and dance and pave your own path and lead and lead and lead. You know what to do. Part of you knows why you came. Forget the details – just close your eyes and live your soul's most exquisite dream. There are so many ways for you to express who you are, so lift your chest, open your heart, and emanate.

*Reach down for the key you've*
*always had and free yourself from*
*the limits and cages that others have*
*imposed on you and put you in.*

And while you're at it, free all of those who you've tried to hold captive for fear that you weren't enough. None of us is truly free to dream if we're holding anyone captive, including ourselves.

You are part of a team that's here to help the healing of humanity. The healing can only fully happen when you first tend to yourself. Those who are resourced can most effectively help. We each take it in turns to give and receive this support through all of life's changing seasons. This is a time that's been whispered of throughout the ages. We're remembering that change is the one constant. I know it can feel disorientating and that it's also difficult to stay connected, but in doing so your presence blesses those who are asleep, hurting, hungry, and separate.

## SOUL INQUIRY

*If you knew it would work out and you weren't worried about what people might think, what would you do, say, or create?*

*How are you most called to spend your precious energy and time?*

## △
# MEET THE MYSTERY MEETING YOU

So often we feel as if we should do something, be somewhere, experience something other than what we're met with. Resist facing what we're faced with. Instead of standing face-to-face with our current experience of life, we reason our way into thinking things should not be as they are. We should not be where we are.

Shapeshifting to avoid what we're served. Losing ourselves in the illusion that it, that we, that life should be different to how it currently is. Keeping time instead of trusting it. Falling out of the arms of Life and choosing instead to hold it all by ourselves. Mistrusting the mystery that's meeting us.

When the mystic encounters something different from what they expect, they know the quickest way out is to find a way to meet the mystery that's meeting them. To lean into what's facing them. To surrender to the great unknown. To surrender to the mysterious pulse of Life. To embrace the season, knowing that soon it will change. To accept what is because it is. To let the tides carry them far out to sea and then when the tides shift, to let them carry them home to ground different than before.

## SOUL INQUIRY

*How can you embrace what's on your path*
*a little more instead of resisting it?*

## △
# KNOWING WHEN TO SURRENDER
# AND WHEN TO PUSH

In many births (literal or metaphorical), there comes a point when the tides change, and we cannot *not* push. Right up to that moment, pushing would be a waste of precious energy, like swimming against the current. And just before this happens the world of and around the becoming mother becomes so still, we can hear a pin drop. A portal opens. An end happens so a beginning can begin.

During my first birth, as my contractions rolled in and out far more intensely than I could ever have imagined, I remember looking to my midwives, desperate for them to answer my questions: 'Should I push? How do I know when to push?' Their response: 'You'll know it's time to push when you can't do anything but push.'

Such an incredible trust they held in a mother's ability to know. Deep down in my cells I *did* know, but I needed to be reminded how to trust this ancient knowing. But I didn't know *until* I knew. And when I knew, I knew with certainty. Isn't that the case with so many things we experience for the first time? We only know when we know. And when we know, there's no way to unknow the knowing.

Of course, just like every life and every death, every labor (literal or metaphorical) is unique. In my second labor, I had more trust in my body's ability to truly know when to surrender and when to push, I'd been through the threshold before. The labor was much longer yet much less intense. I knew not to rush it. I longed to find a way to savor the sacredness of it. To find a way to be in it beyond the pain.

Contractions rolled me in and out of the primordial ocean's waters for more than 40 hours. Some moments thrashing out of my depth. Others calm and crystalline. When the tides shifted, everything got very still. All at once I knew. And everyone in the room knew too. For a moment the world stopped. The gates of Life appeared. I climbed into the birth pool and into the excruciating, indescribable ring of fire. Seconds later, a baby girl and a woman were reborn.

## SOUL INQUIRY

*What are you being called to birth right now?*

*Right now, are you being called to surrender or push?*

△

# FINDING YOUR SOUL'S SONG

A message from the Ancient Grandmothers of the Earth:

Into the dark of night, dear birther of the new dawn, here to assist in a new yet also ancient way for humanity. We, the ancient ones who have been here since the beginning, are beckoning you forth. We never stopped singing you on.

In the heart, you'll find your soul's true dream song. We sang it to you on the day you took your first breath, in recognition of your soul's return. And if you anchor yourself here in the mystical heart, you'll hear that song echo on and on. It will remind you of what you've always known.

This is what it means to remember. This is the dream of your ancestors, celestial and flesh. Your purpose is to listen to your soul's song and then follow its tune. To devote your life to living in harmony with it. When you live from this place, you live your most truthful and joyful life. Anything that helps you stay in harmony with the heart is an indication that it's part of your path.

As you harmonize at a cellular level it brings harmony to more and more. Re-constellating within your system brings harmony to all. As you heal, humanity heals. As humanity heals, you heal. Now more than ever, we're being called to allow that which has been buried, locked away, and silenced to be seen, known, felt, and heard.

*So, sing the song you came here to sing. Follow each note echoing in the four chambers of your heart. Walk in congruence with each beat – it's how you share your medicine.*

This isn't an easy path for you or for the rest of humanity. Some of you may feel as if you're the only ones in your constellation who are doing this work. You're not. Wise ones from your future and your past who did not forget are assisting you every step of the way. You may not see it but if you tune in you might just feel it. Call upon them, positive ones, allies, all the way back and all the way forward.

There's a reason you chose to come to this planet, this family, this body, this time. Your soul chose it. It dreamed it into being. One day you'll look back and see all the sacred threads of your journey of awakening and look on in awe at the magnificent orchestration that's currently and always taking place.

This time in which we're living is one that will be remembered by future souls. This is the great integration. The awakening began long before, but now it needs to be anchored. The world of spirit and matter must return as one. We know that being human right now might be confronting and that it certainly isn't linear. But have faith in the possibility that within you is an intelligent pulse that knows exactly what to do. Let this intelligent pulse beat through you. Let this intelligent pulse direct you.

This isn't the time to analyze. It's the time to surrender. You'll be given all the support and assistance that your soul needs. This doesn't mean it will be easy. Those who have said yes to the path of the soul have said yes to depth. But the deeper you go, the higher you'll eventually soar. And make no mistake, you came here to soar.

You're the ones your grandmothers prayed for. And if you listen in the depths of night at the moment before the sun appears, you'll hear them singing you on.

# the many ones

We are the many Ones.

A l o n e

until we remember how
to be all one together.

Only ever apart when we forget
that we each play a part.

We are the many Ones.
United as One.

# △
# WALKING YOUR SACRED PATH

All the dreams, insights, visions, awakenings, mystical experiences, wisdom, and guidance in the world are pointless without integration, embodiment, and grounded action. I've come to learn and believe that the key to living a mystical, purposeful life is to first develop a relationship with our soul and then act on it in a consistent way. This is what it means to embody our soul's dream. To integrate spirit into matter. To live the soul's waking dream.

I know from my own direct experience (and have witnessed in countless others) the profound shifts that occur when we first prioritize the relationship we have with our soul and then diligently show up and act on its dreams every day. The more we show up to listen to the wisdom within, the easier it becomes to recognize it when it calls. The more we consistently respond to the calls of our soul, the more we trust it.

Listening and acting on the calls of our soul isn't a one-time thing; it's a way of life. It requires that we prioritize the connection, trust the guidance we receive, and act on it every day. So many people stop themselves from living a soul-led life because they're waiting to know the destination before taking the first step. But intuition doesn't work like that. Our soul is always calling us, every moment of every day.

The way to find yourself living in harmony with the sacred pulse of Life is to listen within and embody those calls each day. The Spirit of Life is on your soul's side. It wants to support you as you walk your sacred path.

So, this is your reminder to show up.

To start small.

Bite-sized.

To put one foot in front of the other.

To do one thing every day.

To break things down into achievable tasks.

To truly live your waking dream.

If you do it each day, by the time the Wheel of the Year has turned, you'll be well on your way to living your soul's wildest dream.

You don't need to have it all figured out or know exactly where the path is leading you. You don't have to know every single step along the way before you set out on your great journey. You just need to take the next step.

## SOUL INQUIRY

*What's a baby step you can take to live that*
*dream a little more fully today?*

# soul at the center

We're the weavers, the ones who came to
weave the worlds of spirit and matter back together.
To mend what's been separated and torn apart.
Soul at the center, sacred bridge between heaven and Earth.

One by one as we regulate our nervous systems,
we regulate the nervous systems of humanity,
and our hearts find our way back to the
sacred pulse of the cosmos and the Earth.

We're remembering that we're part
of the ordered Universe.

Our true nature knows what to do,
for we are part of nature and nature has within it
an intelligent pulse that's intrinsic to all of Life.

Nature knows what to do.
And because we're not separate from nature, we do too.

## △
# LED FROM WITHIN

We're the integrators. The cycle breakers. The weavers of the web. On behalf of humanity, we're holding a healing, golden thread. This golden thread was there when we were born, and it will continue pulsing on and on after we're dead. This golden thread is connected to the intelligence of the cosmos. It's always available to guide us, but we can only tap into its intelligence by going within.

External direction will only confuse. The connection must be made from the temple within the portal of your heart. When we connect to this place, we connect to a portal of wisdom so vast that no book or wise one in the knowable or unknowable Universe could ever compare.

No newsfeed or map will lead us to the places that the inner ones can.

No external temple is as sacred as the one we were born with in the center of our hearts.

We're here to bring, embrace, and surrender to change. All awake dreamers are. But to do this we must be led from within. So, we reach out our hands and take hold of the golden thread. And each and every day, we're led.

## SOUL INQUIRY

*Right now, how are you being intuitively led?*

## the weaver

She was a dreamer,
but she was not asleep.
She was a sensitive,
but she was not at all weak.

She was a weaver,
Her life was the thread.
She followed an inner map,
She was always internally led.

# △
# CONNECTING TO THE GOLDEN
# THREAD OF YOUR LIFE

The golden thread is the path of your destiny. The golden thread holds the potential of all that was, is, and could be. The golden thread of your life is always available to guide you, every step of the way, toward your soul's deepest dream. The golden thread is woven throughout all your life experiences. It doesn't always make sense, but with time and perspective you can see the intricate weavings glistening back at you in the middle of your life.

It's never too late to follow the golden thread of your life and you can never be too old. For the golden thread of your life is always within your reach. Whatever your soul is calling you to do will lead you to your golden thread. Wherever you most feel connected to the Spirit of Life is where you'll find your golden thread.

I believe in both destiny and free will. I believe our souls came in with a plan. There are destiny moments plotted along the golden thread of our lives where we can choose to say yes and act on it. This is when our soul's dream becomes a waking one, and suddenly, we find ourselves on our soul's sacred path.

No matter how high and deep your soul has dreamed, without grounded action it cannot be realized. Even the most magnificent creatives, artists, writers, and inventors must show up day after day. Even those whose gifts are innate and extraordinary keep working on their craft daily. They're still living the questions and embodying what they're being called to embody. Courageous enough to believe that they can live their soul's wildest dream.

*This life is but a breath in the timeline of your soul.*
*And you came here to truly live.*

So, keep your heart open through the highs and the lows. Embrace it all. Gather the courage to face your fears and let go of who you thought you were in order to surrender to your becoming. Death is no less alive than birth. Rebirth isn't possible without it.

Trust the changing seasons of your life, for there's medicine waiting for you in every one. A seed doesn't look like a tree. But it holds the potential for it. You're like that too. Your soul chose to be here, in this body, on this planet, at this time. You don't need to know the end destination; you just need to trust that you'll be led.

Before you drew your first breath your soul chose the perfect conditions for your return. It dreamed up the specifics of your great journey this time around. You came here with a plan. All dreamers do. A wish to be brought to life, a dream to be realized. And while this world can be difficult, while the heart can so deeply hurt, it can also be exquisite and glorious. The greatest triumph of a life well lived is to somehow, through the ecstasy and the agony, the grief and the bliss, invite your soul to come all the way in. So that as you exhale your last breath, you can say yes, I've truly lived.

## SOUL INQUIRY

*What is your soul most calling you to do?*

I'm not who I was before.
I'm not who I'll soon be.
Parts of me, of us, are forever dying.
No idea how long we have with each other.

A breath, a season, a lifetime, a year.
Ever-changing beings
living in an ever-changing world.
Forever invited to die and face
death while still fully living.

**These are the death mysteries.**
**These are the birth mysteries.**
**These are the life mysteries.**

The End.

(Also the beginning.)

# △

# RESOURCES

## Therapies and Treatment Methods

**Brainspotting** – a powerful, focused treatment method that works by identifying, processing, and releasing core neurophysiological sources of emotional and physical pain and trauma. **brainspotting.com**

**The Centre for Systemic Constellations (CSC)** – family constellation work focuses on relationships and dynamics within the family system. The CSC offers courses, seminars, and workshops in the UK and internationally. **thecsc.net**

**Dr. Bri's Vibrant Pelvic Health** – Dr. Brianne Grogan is a holistic women's health coach with proven programs for improving pelvic function naturally via body awareness, movement, nutrition, and the mind–body connection. **vibrantpelvichealth.com**

**EFT International** – the world's leading Professional Emotional Freedom Techniques (EFT) organization, offering self-help guides, trainings and a directory of practitioners. **eftinternational.org**

**EMDRIA** – Eye Movement Desensitization and Reprocessing (EMDR) is a psychotherapy method proven to help people recover from trauma and PTSD symptoms. Find out how it works and how to find a therapist. **emdria.org**

**Internal Family Systems Institute** – offers a practitioner directory for those looking for IFS trained providers, and international learning opportunities for those exploring personal growth through IFS. **ifs-institute.com/practitioners**

**Psychology Today** – the world's largest mental health and behavioral science site. Its therapist directory lists verified mental health professionals and treatment centers providing mental health services in 20 countries. **psychologytoday.com**

**Somatic Experiencing International** – a potent method for resolving trauma symptoms and relieving chronic stress. Find a practitioner here: **directory.traumahealing.org**

**SOURCE Process and Breathwork** – breathwork practice to support and empower birthing people, created by pioneering international teacher Binnie Dansby. **binnieadansby.com**

**Tension and Trauma Releasing Exercises (or TRE®)** – a series of exercises that assist the body in releasing deep muscular patterns of stress, tension, and trauma. **traumaprevention.com**

**Trauma informed healing** – healer and teacher Kay Dayton focuses on three therapeutic modalities – brainspotting, TRE, and IFS – to help women process trauma in the brain, nervous system, body, and soul. **kaydayton.co.uk**

# Miscarriage

**The Worst Girl Gang Ever** – a support platform, with private Facebook groups and a free podcast. **theworstgirlgangever.co.uk**

**Tommy's** – the UK's largest pregnancy and baby loss charity, with a dedicated free midwife support line (and special helpline reserved for Black and Mixed Black birthing people). **tommys.org**

**The Miscarriage Association** – the dedicated miscarriage support charity, which has a free helpline, forums, moderated Facebook groups, and online and in-person support groups. **miscarriageassociation.org.uk**

**Miscarriage Australia** – provides information on miscarriage, treatment options, and when and how to seek medical and emotional support. **miscarriageaustralia.com.au**

# Baby and Infant Loss

**Sands** – a charity that supports bereaved parents who have experienced pregnancy or baby loss. It provides a free support helpline, online communities, and in-person and local support groups. **sands.org.uk**

**Petals** – the baby loss counseling charity, offering free counseling to support men, women, and couples through loss. **petalscharity.org**

**The Lullaby Trust** – a charity that offers specialist support for families bereaved by sudden infant death, providing a free helpline, Facebook groups, online meet-ups, and free resources. **lullabytrust.org.uk**

# Postpartum Support

**Pandas** – an organization supporting every parent or network affected by perinatal mental illness, offering resources, a helpline, and support groups. **pandasfoundation.org.uk**

**Postpartum Support International** – provides up-to-date information, resources, and education to support women and birthing people during pregnancy and postpartum. **postpartum.net/get-help/help-for-moms**

**March of Dimes** – offers a variety programs to serve specific maternal and infant health needs throughout the US. **marchofdimes.org**

## Recommended Reading

Carmichael, A. (1992) *Carmina Gadelica: Hymns and Incantations*. Floris Books.

Dana, D. (2020) *Polyvagal Exercises for Safety and Connection*. W. W. Norton & Company.

Dickson, E. and Woodman, M. (1997) *Dancing in the Flames*. Shambhala.

Forest, D. (2014) *The Druid Shaman*. Moon Books.

Grof, S. and Grof, C. (1989) *Spiritual Emergency*. Penguin Publishing Group.

Jenkinson, S. (2015) *Die Wise*. North Atlantic Books.

Johnson, K. A. (2017) *The Fourth Trimester*. Shambhala.

Kent, T. L. (2024) *Wild Mothering*. Atria Books/Beyond Words.

Khan, H. I. (1988) *The Music of Life*. Omega Publications.

Ledwick, H. (2023) *Why Mum's Don't Jump*. Allen & Unwin.

Levine, P. A. (1997) *Waking the Tiger*. North Atlantic Books.

Maté, G. (2019) *When the Body Says No*. Vermilion.

Meddings, N. (2017) *How to Have a Baby*. Eynham Press.

Neumann, E. (2015) *The Great Mother*. Princeton University Press.

O'Donohue, J. (2016) *Beauty: the Invisible Embrace*. Harper Perennial.

Redmond, L. (2018) *When the Drummers Were Women*. Echo Point Books & Media.

Reid, R. (2021) *Reclaiming Childbirth as a Rite of Passage*. Word Witch.

Sjoo, M. and Mor, B. (1991) *The Great Cosmic Mother*. Bravo Ltd.

Sogyal Rinpoche (2008) *The Tibetan Book of the Living and Dying*. Rider.

St. John of the Cross (2003) *Dark Night of the Soul*. Dover Thrift Editions.

Teish, L. (1991) *Jambalaya*. Bravo Ltd.

Underhill, E. and Langdell, T. (2020) *The Mystic Way*. Oxbridge Publishing.

van der Kolk, B. (2015) *The Body Keeps the Score*. Penguin.

Walters, D. (2020) *Kundalini Wonder*. Emergence Education.

Wolynn, M. (2022) *It Didn't Start With You*. Vermilion.

# THE INNER TEMPLE MYSTERY SCHOOL

### with Rebecca Campbell

## Activate your spiritual gifts and embrace your path as a mystic.

▲ Deepen your connection with the Sacred Feminine and the Goddess.

▲ Activate your inherent spiritual gifts.

▲ Unlock ancient secrets not found in books.

▲ Deepen your trust in your intuition.

▲ Express your soul's wisdom with confidence.

▲ Connect with spirit guides and the unseen spirits of nature.

▲ Experience rituals, initiations, ceremonies, and soul journeys.

▲ Join a supportive community of like-minded souls.

▲ Receive accreditation from the CPD Certification Service.

### Is your soul scheduled to go deeper than before?

Join us at the Inner Temple Mystery School:

△

# ACKNOWLEDGMENTS

This book was written over such a vast time and transformative period of my life when I was blessed and touched by so many people without whom these pages would not be what they are.

To my husband and partner in life and work, Craig. You've been there through it all. Thank you for being so willing to build a life that fits our souls. I'm so proud of what we've created together. The Inner Temple Mystery School and these pages would not be the same without you.

To Amy Firth who, as well as being my dear friend, was instrumental in creating The Inner Temple Mystery School Training alongside Craig and me. To my team – Amanda Williams, Alissa Kalina, and Niamh Forshaw-George – who bring such devotion to this work.

To my children, Sunny and Goldie. I cannot imagine my life without you both. You've taught me so much and invited my soul to come all the way into my body. I am so honored to be your mum, and watching you both grow has been the biggest blessing and teaching of my life.

To my mum and dad, who sacrificed so much for my brother and me. I know that things would be much easier if we lived close by and my soul's path was a little more 'normal'! Thank you for always encouraging me to follow my dreams. To my mum, thank you for your support when Goldie had hip dysplasia and for coming over and helping to look after Sunny and Goldie as I was completing this book.

To Binnie Dansby, who has taught me so much. My life was never the same after I walked up that driveway in Oxford. Thank you for all you so generously give and for the countless teachings that you have transmitted deep into my cells. Your support, wisdom, and care during this period of my life was so instrumental. Thank you from the depths of my soul. And to Hollie Holden for being the divine connector that you are.

To my midwife, Julia Duthie, thank you for the exquisite space you held at Goldie's birth and the family constellation work during my pregnancy. Your presence is a real blessing. To Cassie Rosa, my doula for Sunny and Goldie's births. Thank you for your ability to go to the depths and be in deep feminine service. You truly are a sister of the rose.

To Kay Dayton, thank you for your skill and depth throughout the descent. I feel so grateful that our ancestors brought us together in this way! You couldn't have written it! I wish you the deepest joy.

To Sophie Knock, Julia Dvinskaya, Bob Jacobs, Tammy Lynn Kent, Sally Mantle, Yeye Teish, Grandmother Flordemayo, and Andrew Harvey. Each of your gifts and your guidance, depth, and wisdom helped me to move through this hugely transformative period of my life and make sense of it at pivotal moments. Thank you, thank you, thank you.

To my soul brother, Kyle. You are always by my side and always pick up the phone. I'm so deeply grateful for our connection, your love and support, and all the laughs along the way. To Deborah Egerton, thank you for your wisdom, grace, guidance, and friendship. To Meggan Watterson always for the ritual.

To my publisher, Hay House. To Reid Tracy, Michelle Pilley, Margarete Nielsen, Patty Gift, Julie Oughton, Leanne Siu Anastasi, Debra Wolter, and the whole team at Hay House UK. To Amy Kiberd and the huge journey we have been on together! More than most people, you know the many lives this book has had! Thank you for diving deep for this one. I'll always remember that moment on the floor with all the pages around us... 'We've been here before!'

To the spirits of the land here in Glastonbury, who have held and continue to hold me and teach me so much. To my herbalism teacher, Sage Maurer, and my friends Eliza Alloway and Madeline Giles for connecting me with the Gaia School of Healing and reconnecting me to the consciousness of the plants and my ancestors who tended them.

To my friend Tasha Stevens, who taught me so much about foraging and land consciousness. To Sonia Choquette, who taught me how to trust and follow my heart and the unseen world of spirit. To the Four Winds, the Munay-Ki, and the Q'ero of Peru for all of the lessons and remembrance. To Nikki Slade, my dear friend and teacher, thank you for the kirtan training and our connection. I'm so grateful that Shakti keeps weaving us together. To Jim Molyneux, Beth Porter, Rachel Newton, Kerry Andrew, Seckou Keita, Kris Drever, Karine Polwart, and Julie Fowlis for The Lost Words Blessing, which I listened to every day while writing this book.

To my students of The Inner Temple Mystery School Training, thank you for your devotion, dedication, and willingness to see the sacred that's already here, below us, around us, and within us. I have learned so much from what you've shared, channeled, and experienced. To my beloved community, The Sanctuary, thank you for being such a deeply graceful, sacred, safe space to be. I'll be forever grateful and in awe of our corner of the internet and how we're all called together. Thank you from the depth of my soul.

And to you, dear reader, thank you for coming on this journey with me right until the end. I'm so grateful for sharing these pages with you. May you be blessed and bless everyone you meet with your open heart and presence. And may you always remember the dream your soul came to live.

Love,

*Rebecca x*

△

# ABOUT THE AUTHOR

**Rebecca Campbell** is a writer, channel, artist, poet, mystic, and mother. Bridging the worlds of spirituality and creativity, her creations are dedicated to weaving the sacred back into everyday life.

Born in Australia, Rebecca now lives in Glastonbury, UK. As a child, she was fascinated by the great mysteries and at 18, she answered an inner call to take a solo pilgrimage to discover the sacred sites of her ancestry. She's since trained in many disciplines and has had several initiatory awakening experiences, all of which inform her creative process.

Connect with Rebecca:

⊕ rebeccacampbell.me

✉ rebeccacampbell.me/newsletter

▶ @rebeccacampbell

🎙 rebeccacampbell.me/podcast

📷 @rebeccacampbell_author

**f** @rebeccacampbellauthor

CONNECT WITH

# HAY HOUSE
## ONLINE

🌐 hayhouse.co.uk    **f** @hayhouse

📷 @hayhouseuk    **X** @hayhouseuk

▶ @hayhouseuk    ♪ @hayhouseuk

*Find out all about our latest books & card decks • Be the first to know about exclusive discounts • Interact with our authors in live broadcasts • Celebrate the cycle of the seasons with us • Watch free videos from your favourite authors • Connect with like-minded souls*

*'The gateways to wisdom and knowledge are always open.'*

**Louise Hay**

Deep breath, let go, · · · l e a p .

The end is the beginning...